THE POWER OF SMALL HABITS:

ACCOMPLISH TREMENDOUS CHANGES AND TRANSFORM YOUR LIFE WITH THESE 7 SIMPLE VALUABLE HABITS

SIR. CONSTANTINE

11 Small Habits to Big Changes List

(You can't start your day without these...)

This list includes 11 small habits you cannot start or finish your day without that have been personally tested by myself and thousands of people out there and trust me; they do really work!

If you want to want to see big changes in your life, start from here.

To receive your powerful list, visit the link:

www.sirconstantine.com

CONTENTS

INTRODUCTION

Do you have goals you haven't reached yet? Maybe you want to finally lose weight and improve your health. Or maybe you have plenty of great ideas, but no time to work on them. Maybe you're good at starting projects based on your great ideas, but somehow you can't quite get around to finishing them. Do you spend too much time binging on food, watching TV, or scrolling through social media? How many times have you given up your New Year's resolutions by the end of January?

You're not alone! Achieving goals takes self-control and willpower. But relying on these two things, especially willpower alone, won't help you get to where you want to go. It's true that willpower is like a muscle and can be exercised to grow stronger.

However, also, just like a muscle, willpower can become fatigued over time.

To support your efforts and your willpower, you need to add in habits. Habits form the foundation required for you to achieve your goals. In this book, I'll teach you about them. They're the easiest to put in place and to use daily. The great thing about them is that their power compounds the more often they're repeated!

Once you're in the regular habit of performing these steps, you'll see success. The more success, the more confident and motivated you'll be to keep going. By the end, you'll have a virtuous cycle of habits feeding success, which feeds the habits, and so on.

In this book, I've collected the seven simple habits that lead to the path of high achievement. Stacking them on each other is the basis for success in achieving your goals and dreams. All seven are necessary for your journey.

Imagine a ladder that leads from where you are to where you want to go. What happens if some of the rungs are missing? You can't climb the ladder. In the same way, you need to add all seven of these behavior modifications to your daily practice. Each one is a rung on the climb to your ideal life. If you skip one, you won't be able to reach the top.

You're probably wondering how sturdy this ladder is! I built it from all of the experience and knowledge I've obtained over my lifetime. Just like you, in the past, I've been stuck and not sure where to go. My willpower worked for a while, but when I needed it most, it seemed to give out on me. I discovered as I studied that successful people don't rely on their own self-control, as strong as it may seem.

Instead, they relied on routines that weren't very time-consuming, yet the results multiplied over time. Sure, successful people exercise their willpower too, but they use a foundation of habits that they can lean on when the willpower muscle is too tired to get them where they want to go. I began to put these habits in place in my own life and saw the changes I was able to make once I did so.

Once I began to believe that anything is achievable, the pieces of the puzzle fell into place for me. I had to figure it out on my own, but now I know what it takes to be successful, and I'm passing that knowledge on to you. There is a lot of information out there, but all you need to know is what works.

That's what I've included in this book — not a lot of extra padding, just what you need to know to climb the ladder. No matter where you're starting from, you don't need to forge your own path when others have discovered and blazed the trail already. Once you implement the steps in this book, you'll be on the journey of a lifetime (literally)!

If you don't want to transform your life, then you don't need to read this book! It's written for those who are ready and willing to make a change, those who want to lead the life they've always wanted, who have goals they want to achieve. If you're okay with where you are in life and you don't want to improve it in any way, then don't worry about any of these techniques.

On the other hand, what about those who want to take charge of their lives? Those who'd like to stop reacting to what others say and think and forge their own destiny? Those who want to become more self-reliant, more productive, and encounter a life-changing experience that improves their situations? Those people will benefit from reading this book and, more importantly, putting these routines into place in their daily lives.

Want to be in the top 1% that controls 82% of the

wealth in this country? They don't rely only on willpower that can fail them. They have systems in place that support their efforts and all are based on habits.

Thousands of people have transformed their lives by implementing the very techniques you're about to learn about. They're able to effect astonishing results just from consistently making small steps toward their goals every day. The power of these habits to change people's lives over time is absolutely amazing, and you can harness that power too.

Using the procedures that I discuss in this book, you will discover this power for yourself. With my help, you can put these steps to work for you and reap the benefits that result. Those goals that once seemed so impossible and far away? Suddenly they'll seem very achievable once you start stacking these habits for yourself.

You have a choice to make now. You can postpone being the best you that you can be. You can put off reaching the goals that you've always dreamed of. You can delay being more productive and successful. You can stay right where you are, stuck, and feeling hopeless.

However, as Albert Einstein said, "The definition of insanity is doing the same thing over and over and expecting a different result." Why would you want to stay hopeless and stuck and feeling like your goals are too far away even to start?

When all you have to do is start reading! Read and then put each little habit into place on a daily basis. The good news is, you don't have to wait to transform your life. You can start right here, right now.

This book was written for you to be able to implement these routines very easily. Each chapter tells you how to put its topic into action, so you can take each step before moving to the next. Think of a ladder to success. By reading each chapter, you're learning how to build the next rung on the ladder. Implementing each technique is similar to inserting each rung on the ladder. Once the step is there, you can stand on it and start building the next rung. Pretty soon, you'll be able to see the land of your dreams.

Let's get started!

HABIT 1 - CREATE A POWERFUL FOUNDATION

Your mind is the key to your success. If you don't believe you can achieve something, then you're right—you can't. Having the right mindset is the first thing that you need to master. Without the belief that your goals can be reached, even if they're not within easy reach right this instant, you won't be able to put any of the other six habits into place.

Does this seem a little woo-woo or too "out there"? Brain science actually backs this up.[1] You may have noticed that happy, healthy people think about what it is they want and what they must do to get what they want. This kind of thinking makes your brain feel like it's more in control, which makes you happier. When the brain is happy, it releases neurochemicals called endorphins. These give you a sense of well-being, which makes you feel more positive.

The endorphins are a signal from the brain that says, *We like this. Let's do more of this*. The more thinking and planning you do around what you want, the happier the brain is, and the more endorphins it releases. These are the same chemicals that are released when people run ("runner's high") or perform other athletic activities. *We like this; let's do more of this.*

Positive Thinking

Brain science also tells us that our brains can really only focus on one thought at a time. Sometimes it's tempting to think negative thoughts, especially if you've been trying to reach a goal for a while, and you just haven't been able to make it. It's very easy to start thinking that you can't do it, that your willpower isn't strong enough, or that only people with plenty of self-control can do it.

However, once you start attempting positive thoughts and concentrating on them, you'll crowd out the negative ones. One thought at a time means no room for negative ones if you're thinking positively.

The good news is, you can train your brain to come up with positive thoughts! Although they might not be the first ones that come to mind, that's okay. You just have to shove them out of the way by consciously creating more positive thoughts.

An easy way to take care of this is to develop affirmations. Affirmations are positive thoughts that you can easily remember. Repeating them over and over helps cement them in your brain so they can quickly be retrieved if negative thoughts start popping up.

You can also use inspirational quotes. You'll find plenty of them on the Internet, and there are books as well. Maybe you have a favorite author, athlete, or another famous person who you think is inspirational—you can look at quotes from them. Put the quotes in places where you often go: the kitchen, your bedroom or bathroom mirror, your car. Our brains also like a certain amount of repetition. Having the quotes easily accessible when the negative thoughts arrive, as they often do, will help you to focus on the positive and crowd out the thoughts that don't serve you.

Your thoughts are the key to taking action. Positive thoughts are the precursor to positive action.

"Watch your thoughts, they become words; watch your words, they become actions; watch your actions, they become habits; watch your habits, they become character; watch your character, for it becomes your destiny." -Frank Outlaw, *Late President, Bi-Lo Stores*

Everything that you are today is a reflection of what you thought, said, and did in the past. That can't be changed. Nevertheless, if you don't like where you are today, you can start right now to think of positive thoughts. When you're thinking positively, you end up in a positive feedback loop, as illustrated in the above quote.

CULTIVATE OPTIMISM

Happy people are optimistic, and the good news is that people can learn to be more optimistic if that's not their natural state of being. They spend time thinking about what they want, as discussed above.

They're clear about what they want to achieve, and they know they can do it eventually. Just because someone doesn't have the necessary skills now doesn't mean they can't acquire them in the future.

The second thing that positive achievers do is to look for the opportunity or benefit in every failure when things go wrong, as they so often do. If you look for the benefit or the positive in every situation, you'll find it. That helps you to stay positive, which means you don't give up on your goals every time you encounter difficulty.

As strange as it may seem, you can actually decide to be happy. You can work on being optimistic. Assume the good in everyone else too. Sometimes you'll be mistaken, sure, but do have good intentions. They want to help. They're doing the best they can, even if it doesn't always seem like it. If you look for the good in people, just as you do in situations, you'll probably find it, just like you do when looking at your own experiences.

Once you start searching for and finding the benefits in places and things, you'll notice that everything seems to be going better for you. Your mind is releasing those endorphins, so it's providing you positive feedback on your positive feedback. You've started that virtuous circle instead of spiraling down into negativity.

Do you ever feel frustrated or angry? Most of us do! The next time you feel these emotions, think about what's going well in your life. It doesn't have to be anything big. It could be something as simple as feeling clean and refreshed because you just took a shower or that you made it through the big presentation at work without tripping over your own feet and without having spinach stuck in your teeth. If you're angry because your dog ate your shoe, think about how great it is to come home to your dog, who is always so happy to see you.

It's easy to be bombarded with negative news, information, and thoughts. You'll need to (gently) remind yourself to focus on the positive. What's working in your life? What's working in the world? It might take you a minute to come up with something, especially in the beginning. That's okay. Just make sure you find something positive, no matter how far you need to dig for it.

Look for the Opportunity In Failure

Why do you think the motto in many successful

Silicon Valley companies is to fail fast? Because failure provides an opportunity to learn. When everything goes well, you don't actually know what's working and what's a matter of luck for being in the right place at the right time.

However, when you fail, you can look at it as an opportunity to learn. What went wrong, and how can that be prevented next time? Rather than seeing failure as a negative, turn it into a positive. Because we're human, we're going to fail. If you let failure stop you, there's no way you're going to be able to be successful. Failure is a feature of being a person, not a bug. Failing doesn't mean that you're wrong, bad, or a loser. It means that way of doing something didn't work.

Thomas Edison went through hundreds of experiments before he found a light bulb that worked.[2] Imagine if he'd given up after the first failure. Or the tenth. Or the hundredth! He knew there was a way to do it, and he just had to find it.

Using failure as a learning experience can help you feel more confident. Knowing that you're going to fail helps you avoid taking it personally. Learning from it gives you the confidence to try something else. Bottom line; the more confident you are, the more successful you're going to be.

Confidence is another example of a virtuous cycle and a positive feedback loop. When you're certain that you can achieve what you want, you take more actions that lead to success. The more your actions pay off, the more confident you are that you are effective, and so you take even more action.

NEGATE NEGATIVITY

Our own minds are a great place to start when we're trying to set the foundation for success by creating the right mindset. Nonetheless, there are other factors that influence us as well that we should take into account.By some measures, people who watch television news are the most fearful in America.[3] Now that cable television has introduced the idea of 24/7 news, that space has to be filled. What grabs people's attention? The heart-warming tale of a fire-fighter who rescued a cat from a tree? Nope! It's a crime or other bad news. Humans are particularly attuned to negative information, and television has to sell ad space. A famous journalism mantra is "If it bleeds, it leads."

Crime has actually decreased over time, but you wouldn't know it from TV. Also, now that the internet allows for global journalism 24/7, we're also "treated" to the spectacle of bad news from all over the world. Even more negative energy that takes up space in our heads.

We're also influenced by the people we know. Jim Rohn has said we're the average of the five people we hang around with most. That might not be exactly right, but it is true that the people you hang around with matter for your success. Especially the ones you're around the most.

If you're trying to lose weight, for example, who do you think you should be spending time with? Someone who's not interested in eating healthy and working out? Or someone who keeps themselves in good shape? Those who are trying to be more successful at work will do better with others who are career-minded. Less spending time with the guys hanging out on the sofa playing video games and eating pizza and more with other young professionals who get together to network and share information. You might not want to dump your long-time friends just because they don't have the same ideas about success as you do, but you can limit the time you spend with them and expand the time you spend with other people who share your ambitions. It's also true that friends and needs change over time, so don't feel bad about arriving at a place where you want support for your dreams.

When you begin to spend time with people whose goals align with yours, you'll find that thinking positively becomes easier. It doesn't take as much willpower to find things that are working or a positive thought to crowd out the negative one that just arrived in your head. Being surrounded by other people who are also trying to think positively, who are also looking for the good in their surroundings, helps put you in the right frame of mind. In other words, make your environment as positive as you possibly can. This makes developing the right mindset so much easier compared to having to fight through a sea of negativity. No one really needs to watch television news, especially if you spend any amount of time online. If you do think you need to watch it, choose a short period of time to watch and then turn the TV off. You might even want to counter right away by following up with an inspirational story or reading the biography of someone you find inspiring rather than leaving the negativity to fester.Think about the people you spend the most time with. They might be friends, or they might be colleagues or family. Do they support your goals and dreams? Sometimes people are threatened when others close to them begin improving. Your spouse may feel worried that you'll lose interest in them if you lose weight, and they don't. A work colleague might be threatened if you start trying to improve your career moves, etc.. Make sure the people you choose to be with genuinely support your efforts and have similar goals themselves.

THINK LONG-TERM

Anyone who's tried to lose weight in the past knows how difficult it is! You know that eventually, you want to get to a certain weight, or level of fitness, or other measures of health. That's your long-term goal, and you're probably pretty clear about it. But in the short-term, the doughnuts in the break room are tasty. Or you've had a very long, difficult day, and it is so much easier to reach for the junk food in the cabinet or order a pizza than to craft a healthy meal.The problem is, of course, that no one can just jump right to their ideal long-term result. That goal is achieved only by doing small things right day after day. It's easy to get discouraged when the results don't come in the short-term. Spend a day eating right, and the scale barely budges. Deliver a terrific presentation at work, but the promotion doesn't come right away. Come up with a great idea for a start-up business, but the money doesn't come flooding in.

Gary Vaynerchuk, a well-known entrepreneur, noted that success takes time. Years. But it comes with being speedy on a daily basis, getting the meetings, presentations, sales calls, etc. right.[4] You do have to grind in the short-term and let the results play out over the long-term.

Consider investing. Warren Buffett is one of the most successful investors of all time. Thousands of people flood into Nebraska every year when he gives his public talk. Investors all over the world read the letter he writes at the end of every year. He doesn't go in for the latest speculation, and he doesn't gamble on the newest thing.

What he does is read the filings that companies have to make with the SEC and determines whether they're a good value. That's all. It takes a lot of patience to go through the filings, and he's thinking not just about whether the company will do well over the next year, but whether its long-term opportunity is valuable.

In order to think long-term, it helps to really visualize the goal. This isn't woo-woo stuff either. It's backed by science. When we truly "see" in our mind's eye what we want to achieve, our brain thinks it's really happening. Neurons start building new pathways to accommodate this new action.

In other words, visualization is very powerful. Athletes use this technique all the time. They view themselves swimming down the lane and winning the race. They mentally rehearse their free throws, seeing the ball swishing through the hoop.

You don't have to be an athlete to benefit from it. You can visualize what your life looks like after you've achieved your fitness goal, won the promotion or started the business. The more detail you can use, the more your neurons begin to form a new pathway.

Depending on what works for you, you might think about creating a vision board for your goal(s), keep an inspiration journal, and visualize your grand plans.

.   .   .

CHAPTER ONE SUMMARY

- The first rung on the ladder to success is having the right mindset of positivity and optimism. Both can be learned and exercised.
- If you think you can't do something, you're right. Cultivate positive thinking and a positive environment to achieve your goals.
- Consciously find the benefit in all situations.
- Use affirmations to help crowd out negative thinking.
- Find inspirational quotes and people.
- Turn off the TV news.
- Surround yourself with others who support you and your goals.
- Think about what is going well in your life.
- Be grateful for what you have and consider a gratitude journal.
- Use failure as a learning tool and get comfortable with it.
- Recognize that failure is a feature of life.
- What lessons does each failure have to teach you?
- Think long-term and visualize your goals.

- Do the small things every day to reach your goal.
- Visualize your goal in detail.
- Use a vision board or journal to help solidify your vision.

IN THE NEXT CHAPTER, YOU WILL LEARN ABOUT SELF-discipline and how to delay gratification.

*A*n important thing to know about self-discipline is that it doesn't necessarily mean that you're harsh or hard on yourself. It just means that you control your own actions without letting other people's reactions, or even your own, negatively affect the way that you respond. It helps you stick to the path when things get rough and cut down on procrastination and laziness while you're trying to achieve your goals.

Successful people, including athletes, business owners, writers, and investors, find self-discipline to be a key habit as they work to reach their own goals. Olympic athletes and top pro basketball players don't give up when things get difficult. They don't spend the bare minimum of time practicing their sport. In fact, they're more likely to stay in the gym longer than their compatriots. In addition, they don't load up on junk food during competition season because that doesn't get them the results they want. You've probably heard the stories about all the executives who rise at 3 or 4 in the morning. Unless you're a true morning lark, that takes some serious self-discipline. But they do it because mornings are a productive time, and this allows them to maximize that time. They also have many demands, so early waking provides more useful hours in the day, as late evening hours aren't productive for most people who work in an office.

THE IMPORTANCE OF SELF-DISCIPLINE

Everyone faces obstacles in life. They're different for different people, but they do exist, and it's very easy to give up in the face of these obstacles, especially when it's not immediately clear how they can be surmounted. Without the self-discipline to keep going, reaching any goal is pretty much impossible. Giving up is easy, but consistently pushing oneself is not. Once self-discipline becomes a habit, things do get easier. When routines are established, they're easier to stick to. It's the implementation of new habits and new routines that is more difficult.

Remember your high-school physics class? Hopefully, it's not a terrible memory! You may recall the concept of inertia. An object at rest tends to stay at rest, and an object in motion tends to stay in motion (at least when we ignore friction). Once you're in a routine, in motion toward your goal, you'll tend to stay in motion. That is unless friction gets in the way! Self-discipline can help you to reduce that friction to keep you in motion on your journey.

However, it also takes some force for that object at rest to get into motion. It's the same with the new daily habits that you're working on. If you're not doing these things right now, it'll take a bit of force to start using them every day. That force is self-discipline.

Suppose you usually wake up at 7 A.M. every day, and your goal is to be more physically fit. You determine that you'll need to wake up at 5:30 A.M. instead, which will give you time to work out and do what you need to do in the morning. So, you set your alarm. Does that take care of it? Is it setting the correct time for your alarm? Of course not! It's a step in the right direction. After all, if you're used to waking up at 7, there's no way you're going to start off waking naturally 90 minutes earlier. You'll need some help.

In this case, the alarm isn't the one who has to actually get up at 5:30 A.M. in order to be successful. You're the one that has to get out of bed and go work out early in the morning. The first few times the alarm goes off, you are probably not going to want to get up and go. Your first instinct is likely either to turn the alarm off completely or to hit the snooze button.

How do you actually get out of bed at 5:30? Discipline. Your goal is to be physically fit, and it requires exercise, which requires an earlier wake time. You'll need the discipline to get up and do what you need to do because you're (literally) going from a state of rest to a state of motion that'll require a little extra force from your self-discipline.

Over time you'll adjust so that waking at 5:30 A.M. isn't such a heavy lift. After you've done it for some time, you'll no longer be a person who wakes up at 7. You're a person who wakes up at 5:30. It's part of your identity. You're in motion! Also, over time you'll figure out a routine that makes the early morning easier. You'll learn to set out your workout clothes or bag the night before, so you don't have to deal with it. You'll find that the workout is easier with no food first or that you need a small snack before you get to it, and you'll learn to prep accordingly. This is the friction-reducing part to help you stay in this positive, forward motion.

Self-discipline also helps you to take control of decisions, so you can make better ones. Rather than debating how many cookies you can have while you're trying to get fit, you can skip them entirely.

Who should you be spending time with? Being in control of yourself means that you can objectively look at the people you hang out with and decide if they are helping you in your quest for success. If not, you'll be able to spend less time with them or even no time at all, depending on the relationship.

How to Be More Self-Disciplined

In some ways, it's like a muscle—the more you exercise self-control, the stronger it becomes. You can also support it by creating an environment where it's less likely to be fatigued. Here are five things that you can do to create a habit of self-discipline in your life.

1. Identify your weaknesses.

There's no point in putting together healthy habits when there are things that sabotage you, and you either don't know about them or want to pretend they're not there. They are there. Own up to them, and it'll make avoiding or working around your weaknesses much easier.

For people trying to be healthier, weakness is often a food trigger. They're also some of the easiest to avoid. Can't stop at one potato chip or cookie; you have to eat the whole bag? Don't let the bags come in the house, and don't buy them to keep in the car or office either. Are steak and potatoes a big temptation? Buy a smaller plate to eat from, and don't go back for seconds. If there's a dish at a restaurant that you always get and you know it clogs your arteries as soon as you take that first yummy bite, avoid the restaurant.

It's the same with alcohol. If you know you drink the entire six-pack, buy a single bottle instead, or just avoid it altogether.

It gets a little tougher when the trigger isn't so easily avoided. Maybe when someone at work is angry or upset with you, it really upsets you. This is often a mentor, supervisor, or other authority figures.

It could also be your habit of mindlessly scrolling the feed on Instagram. You know that in order to publish your best-selling novel, you have to… well… write it first. But there you are, two hours into your social feed and not a word written.

Social media or other computer time-wasters like video games are also pretty easy to workaround. There are all kinds of apps that will let you shut off certain websites and apps during specific times or whenever you're trying to work. You could also try putting the phone down (which you should do periodically anyway). Shut off the wifi so you can't surf while you're writing.

2. Know your goals and have a plan.

It's very hard to think long-term and set aside these short-term temptations when you don't know what you're trying to achieve. What's the point of not eating a yummy cookie? Or not spending two hours enmeshed in the drama of someone you don't even know via your social feed?

If you want success, what does that mean to you? Does it mean lowering your blood sugar to avoid

Type II diabetes? Does it mean losing 20 pounds or putting on 20 pounds of muscle? Is it reaching the C-suite in a corporation (CEO, CIO, COO, etc.)? Is it launching your own business and selling your product around the world? Is it writing a bestselling book and going on tours and TV shows?

Whatever it is, visualize it, as discussed in Chapter One. Know what it looks like and the steps you need to get there. To have a bestselling book, you need to write a book and also create an author platform that grabs people's attention and gets you on the TV shows you want.

3. Use your head.

Mindset, mindset, mindset! You'll find this idea popping up throughout this book, because just like success, if you think you can't be self-disciplined, then you can't. You need to know that you can, in order to achieve it.

Remove those mental obstacles about willpower! If you think you have a large reserve of willpower, then that's what you've got. Think positive about your ability to be self-disciplined and to stay in control. Visualization works for more than just your overall big goals. You can use it to manage situations that are A, likely to emerge, and B, likely to derail your plan unless you counteract them.

For example, you know that you need to avoid drinking heavily at happy hour because you have a presentation the next day that you hope will give you visibility to senior management. Rather than hoping you don't drink heavily (or eat heavily, which also has some bad effects the next day), prepare for happy hour, assuming you have to go because you might not, and skipping it might be better for you.

Decide ahead of time that you will have some water or soda before your first alcoholic drink or appetizer nibble. Visualize yourself standing with a glass of water in your hand as you talk, skipping the cookies at the end of the table, sipping the alcoholic drink slowly, or eating only a little.

Rehearse tough situations in your head, and picture yourself overcoming the obstacles you know are headed your way. This will make the discipline do what you need to do so much easier.

Reward yourself too. Anticipation can have very powerful benefits. You'll need to choose rewards that don't get in the way of your overall goals, of course. If you want to lose 50 pounds, don't treat yourself to a molten lava cake after you've lost 10 pounds! Maybe try a massage, or a book you want to read, or a podcast you've been dying to listen to.

Don't let failure stop you in your tracks. Acknowledge that something went wrong. Just as discussed in Chapter One, find the lesson. If you gain 2 pounds one week instead of losing them, maybe you drank more soda than you thought, or you went out to eat three nights in a row, and you recognize you didn't choose wisely. Acknowledge that you did eat the entire bag of potato chips.

Beating yourself up about it is counter-productive. You're not going to achieve success by feeling bad about yourself or what you've done. Find the lesson and decide to learn it. Then move on.

4. Keep it simple.

Set yourself up for success. Reduce the friction wherever you can to help you stay in motion toward your goal. Keep the junk food and booze out. Leave your phone in another room to charge while you're working or reading, so you're not constantly interrupted by notifications. These new habits can sometimes be tough, so break them down into smaller, bite-sized pieces. Make the implementation easy with small habits.

Losing 50 pounds is a lot, but 2 pounds a week is doable. What has to happen to lose 2 pounds? Avoid junk food. Exercise for a certain amount of time every day. Those are small, bite-sized habits that will ultimately get you to the big goal.

5. Eat well.

Nobody ever got to the C-suite by being hangry all the time! Most of us don't need a lot of calories, and you can find nutritious ways to get the calories you need. Here again, it's important to set yourself up for success.

Know you're working late one week? Prep enough food the weekend before. Or have easy, healthy go-to meals ready in the cabinet or freezer. Manage your blood sugar, so you're not cranky or constantly struggling with its ups and downs.

We'll go into more detail about how to eat right for success in Chapter 6. For the moment, just make sure you're in the habit of having something prepared to deal with hunger pangs during the day.

. . .

HELP YOUR WILLPOWER LAST LONGER DURING the Day

1. Be consistent.

Practice these suggestions every day. The more consistent you are, the easier it is to ingrain the habits. It's true with all the habits. Especially at the beginning, it's necessary to make sure that you are consciously and deliberately doing what you need to do. If your goal is to start your own business, a daily goal might be to send out a certain number of prospecting emails. Every day, that practice is ingrained into your routine.

Then, it actually becomes easier to be self-disciplined! When you send out ten emails by 9 A.M. every day for a month or so, it will actually feel a bit strange not to send out those emails. You've become someone who sends out ten prospecting emails every morning. Now it's who you are!

2. Get enough rest.

You need to sleep to replenish your willpower stores. Your body undergoes physical changes when it doesn't get enough rest, which has negative consequences. We'll talk about what happens to the body while you're sleeping in more detail in Chapter 5.

As far as willpower goes, your body feels sluggish and needs more energy when you don't get enough sleep, which means you'll be hungry more often. This isn't helpful for most people, and especially not those who are trying to be healthy.

The quickest hit of energy that your body can absorb is glucose. This is why marathoners and ultramilers carry sugar in the form of gels or even candy bars. You won't be craving a nice, healthy salad or even some lean chicken when you don't get enough rest. Your body wants carbs, especially sugar.

3. Say no.

You might not be able to say no to something your boss or someone in authority wants you to take care of, but if a colleague or friend wants you to do something that does not get you to your goals, just say no.

Being effective and successful means that you can't do everything. No one has that kind of bandwidth available. You must focus on what you need to do to reach your goals. Lots of people will have lots of requests for you to help them. Sometimes what they ask might be good for you in the long-term, so you say yes. However, if not, say no, and you don't need to make excuses. Remember, "No" is a complete sentence.

4. Make sure you do the necessary tasks first.

Because self-discipline is like a muscle, it can get fatigued over the course of a day, leading to bad decisions as evening approaches. It's best if you don't make too many decisions during the day, but that's not always possible.

Why do you think Silicon Valley leaders wear the same clothes, or at least the same style, day in and day out? Why do they eat the same food all the time? Rather than using up willpower reserves early in the day trying to figure out what to wear or eat, they've made one decision that frees them from having to make the same one over and over again.

Another way to handle this is to make some decisions the night before, like what you're wearing to work and what lunch you'll be bringing. Then, the next day you have a little more brain space available.

Another important decision that successful people make is to get the hardest tasks done first before willpower starts to deplete. Not only do you avoid procrastinating on important tasks, but you also get a little boost of confidence. You've completed the thing you dreaded, and you made it through unscathed. Not bad!

5. GET COMFORTABLE BEING UNCOMFORTABLE.

If your goal was easy to reach, you'd be there already, wouldn't you? The very nature of the success you're trying to achieve means you can't take the easy way out or do what's comfortable for you. If being successful was comfortable, you wouldn't be reading this book. You'd already be there.

Being able to tolerate discomfort not only helps you grow as a person, but it'll also help motivate you. Once you discover that you're a person who can do difficult things—because you pushed through your comfort zone straight into discomfort—you'll become more confident. The more you can take on small things and win, the more self-assured you feel about taking things on.

You'll grow into the positive mindset we discussed in Chapter One. The more you tolerate discomfort to do the things you want and need to do, the more obvious it will be that you can achieve your goal because you've already had some success along the way.

. . .

DELAY YOUR GRATIFICATION

Delay pleasure now. Feel more lasting satisfaction later. This part of self-discipline goes back to the long-term thinking discussed earlier in the chapter. When you're feeling angry and you chomp on a bag of potato chips, you're gratifying that need instantly, but when you decide not to chow down, you're delaying gratification. You'll feel great when you've lost the weight instead of the temporary satisfaction you feel while you're chewing the chips.

Not eating the chips won't cause your weight to drop immediately. It will, however, help to prevent gaining weight. You're delaying the satisfaction of having it right now, to the future, when the gratification is usually longer-lasting.

It may seem pretty obvious delaying gratification with food: avoid now, reap the benefits of being healthier later. Overcoming addiction is similar: abstinence now, release from the substance (or whatever the addiction is) later. Having a budget (or spending plan, if you prefer) balances short-term needs or quick hits from shopping, with the long-term goals of a comfortable retirement or buying a new house. When you're trying to reach any goal, you'll need to break that habit of instant gratification.

However, success doesn't come right away. You can't get success by touching an app on your phone. You have to put in the work, whatever is necessary to get to where you want to be. You'll have to skip some happy hours with friends in order to create a presentation that will help you land the promotion you want.

You'll have to stop scrolling through social media and enjoying that little dopamine hit every time someone likes one of your posts in order to sit down and write your bestseller.

Have you heard of the marshmallow study? A scientist studied a group of small children. Each was placed in a room with a marshmallow and told if they could wait until the adult returned, they would get an additional marshmallow. Those who were able to wait, to delay gratification, did better in school and socially than the ones who didn't.[1] This research has held true as the kids have had follow-ups for 40 years. Don't worry. All hope is not lost, even if you're pretty sure you would have snatched that treat as soon as the adult left. You can get better at this skill, just as you can other measures of self-control.

The researchers also split the kids into two groups. One group was told they would get a small treat, like a box of crayons, which they never received. The other group was told they would get the treat, and they did. Needless to say, the kids who had a reliable experience were better at delaying their gratification. They'd been primed for the treat being there.

Nonetheless, the other group was primed to show that promises are unreliable. Of course, they snagged the marshmallow: what proof did they have that additional treats would actually be forthcoming as promised?[2]

This demonstrates that context and experience affect self-control. You may have grown up in a household where promises were unreliable, but you're an adult now. You can start training yourself to be reliable so that your brain understands that the reward will be forthcoming. (Another reason to reward yourself as discussed above!)

The best way to do this is to start small, with something so easy you almost can't not do. Do that every day. You could try a habit tracker where you check off each day if you completed the task. Our brains really hate when we break patterns, so having a physical reminder of what you're doing can really help you to stay on track.

In addition, in the marshmallow study, the researchers found that the kids who were able to delay gratification employed tactics to distract themselves from the tempting marshmallow.

They didn't just sit and stare at it. So can you, use some strategies to help you delay gratification.

Remove temptation when you can, for example, and keep the vision of your goal in front of you, so you have a reason to avoid the chips, not to buy the video game, or go home and read your inspirational book instead of hanging out at the sports bar.

You have a goal, and keeping it front and center will help you to avoid the trap of instant gratification.

This is why you need that very clear vision of what success looks like to you. Otherwise, it's too easy to succumb to the chips.

.

.   .   .

CHAPTER TWO SUMMARY

- The habit of self-discipline is necessary for success.
- Self-control is like a muscle; you can train and strengthen it.
- Identify your weaknesses and remove them where possible.
- Visualize your goals in great detail; create a vision board and/or write about them.
- Stay in a positive mindset.
- Reward yourself for small wins.
- Mentally rehearse ahead of time how you will handle stressful situations.
- Keep going after failure.
- However, also like a muscle, self-control gets fatigued. You can learn to support your willpower habit.
- Be consistent and stay in your habit.
- Prioritize sleep.
- Say "no" to things that don't serve you and your goal.
- Prioritize tasks so you get the hard ones out of the way when you still have willpower reserves.

- Practice getting comfortable with discomfort.
- Delaying gratification is important to success, and the marshmallow test shows that this can be learned as well.
- Make sure your goal is front and center, so you always see the reason for delaying gratification—your ultimate goal.
- Practice being consistent so your brain learns that promised rewards do come.

IN THE NEXT CHAPTER, YOU WILL LEARN HOW TO JOIN the 3% of people who actually set their goals.

HABIT 3 - LET'S SET THE GOALS

*I*f you don't know what success means to you, how will you know if you're successful? You need to know what goals you want to reach in order to maximize your potential. If you don't know what you're trying to achieve, this chapter will help you learn how to set goals and, equally important, how to design a plan to get you there.

"The ability to set goals and make plans for their accomplishment is the 'master skill' of success." - Brian Tracy

---

If you obtain the skills for setting and achieving goals, you'll be in a very elite group! Only 3% of Americans write down their goals, and only 1% review them daily.[1] If goals are so important to success, then why do so few people manage to have written goals?

It's likely due to some combination of factors of the following five reasons.

1. People aren't "serious" about success.

When you talk to those who have achieved their goals, you may find some have always known what they wanted to do and were driven to take those steps, but others often say that their success didn't happen until they "got serious." When you get tired of being sick and tired, that's when the action starts to happen for a lot of people.

2. They don't understand how important goals actually are.

Many of those who understand the power of goals grew up in a goal-oriented household, where their family talked about goals, what goals them-selves had, and their importance. But if like me, you come from a family that didn't discuss goals or understand how they're the key to success, you didn't grow up with that knowledge. For this reason, so many of us are young adults (or older!) before we start thinking about goals and how to achieve them.

3. They don't know how to set goals.

Most schools don't teach this skill, and if you come from a family as described above, like mine, you didn't learn it from your parents either.

4. Fear of rejection.

Many of us grow up in environments where goals might have been frowned upon, or you might have been told you could never achieve them. No wonder people don't set goals, especially when the people who most influence us in childhood are the ones telling us that we can't do what we want to do.

It's usually done by parents who don't understand goals and their misguided attempt to prevent their children from being harmed.

Unfortunately, it impedes a lot of us when we want to achieve some success. Being rejected by family, peers, or colleagues is not a positive environment! Because of this, you might not want to tell anyone about your goals, especially while they're in the early stages. That way, you won't be derailed by rejection.

5. Fear of failure.

Having a goal, especially a big one, does require some courage. Although, as we discussed in Chapter One, failure is necessary for growth. However, the same criticism many of us received in childhood and maybe even early adulthood, which led to fear of rejection, leads to a fear of failure too. After all, for many of us in school, what happened when we failed? We were scolded, maybe even punished. It's understandable that many of us carry a fear of failure with us.

When you realize that failures are inevitable along the way, that helps to take some of the dread away. Particularly when you use them for learning experiences. The first time you are able to fall and get right back up and keep moving, you'll realize that failure doesn't have to stop you.

WHY GOALS NEED TO BE WRITTEN DOWN

You might already have a goal in mind. Why is it

important to write it down? In other words, why is joining the 3% key to achieving your success?

There's a big difference between having something in your head only and writing it down. Once it's on paper, you can actually see and evaluate it. A list of your goals, or your goal and your plan to achieve it, helps to keep you motivated.

When you want to eat that bag of chips or go to happy hour with the guys the night before the big presentation at work, it's easy to fall into the instant gratification trap. Part of your brain is warning you, vaguely, that you shouldn't. Nevertheless, it might be too late in the day for you to care, or you might even be feeling rebellious. You're an adult, and you can eat ice cream and cake for breakfast if you want to!

Having the goals already written down gives you a little boost. The language in your head changes from "I shouldn't" to "I don't want to do this behavior because it interferes with something I want more." That's a powerful incentive to put down the chip bag or to sit down with the biography of your favorite inspirational person.

In fact, it can be very helpful at the beginning of the day, when you're still fresh, to rewrite your goals.

This directs your brain's attention to where you want it to focus and will make it easier for you to overcome temporary temptations as you move forward in the process.

How to Set Goals in a **SMART** Way

The best way to achieve your goals... is to make them achievable. Focus on the process, not on the outcome. You may have heard of SMART goals, which will help you to stay on the path to success. It's good to have a *big, hairy, audacious* goal that maybe right now doesn't seem like you can reach it, but in order to get there, you need some shorter-term goals that may be a bit of a stretch, but still within reach.

SMART stands for Specific, Measurable, Achievable, Relevant, and Time-bound.

Specific goals help you key in on the steps you need to take in order to get to where you want to go. That way, the goal isn't so vague that you have no idea where to start.

The way to know if your goal is **measurable** is to see if there's a point at which you know you've achieved it. For example, suppose you think your goal is to be physically fit. How do you know when you've achieved that goal? It isn't measurable. Instead, try something like being physically fit enough to be able to run a marathon. That's measurable.

Achievable is another component of successful goal-setting that's personal to you. If you weigh 200 pounds, losing 150 pounds isn't achievable. If you weigh 500 pounds, that same weight loss can be achieved. However, losing it in 2 months is not possible.

The point of a goal is to help you get to where you want to go and to do so while staying in harmony with your values and ethics. That's why the goal must be **relevant**. If your overall goal is to be promoted into the C-suite of a company, then a goal to read biographies of all the presidents is not relevant. On the other hand, connecting with ten people in your industry every day may be.

Finally, nearly everyone needs deadlines to be successful, so the goals must be **time-bound**. Life happens, as they say. It's tough to stay on track when you're constantly putting out fires at work and/or raising a family. Timelines help you stay accountable to your goals and encourage you to actually do the work you need to do to be successful.

OTHER DAILY GOAL HABITS TO HELP YOU STAY ON Track

You'll find that a lot of the habits we discussed in earlier chapters come into play in others! There are a number of common steps to the habits of success, like rewarding yourself and visualizing your success. Here are some other ways that you can support your goals.

1. Make a list.

The power of writing things down also includes the fact that with our fast-paced lives, it's hard to remember everything. Trying to recall what you need to do only serves to distract your brain. Make a list and make life easier for your brain.

2. Minimize distractions and clutter.

This goes for the top of your desk, your office, your phone, and your laptop or tablet—whatever you use to work on.

Having a lot of physical objects on your desk makes

it hard for most people to concentrate on their tasks. Clearing it off can help you focus. The same goes for apps and icons on your phone and laptop. A messy interface is the same as a messy desk. Organize your files into folders, whether they're on your physical desk or on your screens.

While you're working, you should have notifications disabled. That includes; phone, social media, email, anything that pops into your field of vision, buzzes, vibrates, or makes some sort of noise. If you need to shut your phone off to do that, then do it. (Your phone should periodically be shut off and restarted anyway, as should all electronic tools.)

It's too easy to be distracted by an email that comes in or a friend who posts to your social media feed, but once you're distracted from your main task, it takes time to get back to work. When that happens multiple times a day, you end up wasting a lot of time on unimportant trivia that doesn't move you toward your goal.

3. Make the most of mornings and weekends.

Mornings are the most productive time of the day for many people. It's particularly hard for those who are juggling a full-time job and a family to find the time to work on their goals.

If that's you, consider waking up earlier. (I know, if you don't love mornings, it's no fun.) But think about how much work you can get done when your phone's not ringing, your kids aren't up, and no one's emailing you urgently because they didn't do their job right.

If you've ever arrived at work early, you know how peaceful it is, and you've probably been amazed at how much you were able to accomplish. Try the same thing at home.

Although we typically think of weekends as time off, especially those working a 9-5 job, they're also a terrific time to work on your goals. Sitting around in front of a screen may sound relaxing, but your brain (and your body) actually don't like it. Your brain wants some stimulation, and sitting all day is bad for your health.

You can take time Sunday night to prep for the week ahead, and then Monday isn't so full of chores. Set out your outfit, make your lunches and maybe even dinners for the next week, plan when you're going to spend time with your friends and family, or working on your goals. You'll be amazed by how productive the week is!

4. Act 'as if.'

This habit is similar to visualization but not exactly the same. You will need to have a very clear idea of your goal because you need to know what kind of person you want to be.

For example, suppose your goal is to be physically fit (a true goal would be more specific than this, but bear with me here). What does a physically fit person do?

They don't sit and play video games all night. Maybe they do play games, but only the active kind. Physically fit people get up early enough to make sure they workout in the morning before the rest of the day starts. No matter what happens, they got their workout in. They go on walking meetings at work instead of sitting with coffee and a donut.

Once you know what people who have achieved the success you want to do during the day, you can act as if you're already the person you want to be.

You want to be a person who takes walking meetings, so you suggest it the next time someone wants to get together. You want to be a person who plays active games, so you find a recreational league or even an active video game and start. You set your alarm earlier in the morning in order to wake up early enough to work out.

You may not be physically fit yet, but you can act as if you are. There's no reason to delay picking up these great habits.

When your ambition is to get into the C-suite, you need to act as if you have the job you want. (Which doesn't mean being arrogant and ordering people to get you coffee!) It might entail dressing better. Unless you work in the tech industry, you'll find most execs wear suits.

People in the C-suite review their progress every day and make plans for the next. Act as if you're an exec and do the same.

5. Find help.

In addition to being surrounded by people who support your goals, you'll need some who actively help you get to where you want to go. Sometimes this type of help comes in the form of a mentor, someone who's been where you are and achieved success themselves.

Depending on your goal, you may or may not find other people who've made the same journey you want to make. You can still find mentors in successful people, even if they don't have your exact background or goal.

Likewise, although a personal mentor is very helpful, you might find someone who is a celebrity or well-known in their field. In cases such as this, you won't be able to make much direct contact with them. Nevertheless, you can still follow them on social media and read what they have to write.

You will probably benefit from an accountability partner or mastermind group. They'll ask you where you are in achieving your goals. If you don't manage to make a deadline, they'll help you to figure out why. You do the same for them, and the partnership works for both of you.

6. Manage your time wisely.

With our always-on 24/7 culture, everyone has a lot going on. Successful people don't do everything that everyone wants them to do. They also don't do everything they themselves want to do! When you're trying to add important tasks and habits that will get you to your ideal life, some of the other tasks necessarily need to fall off the to-do list.

There are some obvious places to start, such as time wasted on screens: video games, television, phones, social media, etc.. However, once you've cut those out or minimized them, you may still need to manage your time. There are a couple of ways to think about this.

- Pareto Principle

You might remember this from science. In most endeavors, 20% of the effort results in 80% of the results. It might be 20% of clients or 20% of your tasks that get you the best results.

Right now, you might not know what the 20% is, so you'll need to do a little investigating. This is relevant to your goal, as well. Look at everything you're doing to achieve the goal. Look into past results if you can, and if you're just starting, you'll need to try different methods to see what works.

For example, if you're trying to put on muscle, you're probably lifting weights, trying to increase your protein intake, and maybe some other things. Which of these seems to have the biggest effect on your goal?

These can change over time, too. At first, it might be the higher protein intake that helps you increase your muscle definition, but then that effect flatlines. Now, you need to focus more on lifting weights.

Whatever isn't working or isn't having much of an effect, don't concentrate on it

- Importance vs. Urgency Matrix

Imagine a 2x2 matrix, with one side being *Urgency* and the other being *Importance*. You'll end up with four quadrants: Important and Urgent, Important and Not Urgent, Not Important and Urgent, and Not Important and Not Urgent.

Consider your activities. If any of them fall into the Not Important and Not Urgent category, delete them. Don't even bother with them. Life is too short. (Just make sure they're also neither important nor urgent for anyone else.)

Try to make sure that most of your activities are in the Important and Not Urgent box, which will be long-term and strategic activities.

Important & Urgent means that you're dealing with a lot of short-term crises or putting out fires. Not Important and Urgent are distractions and interruptions, which you want to avoid as much as possible.

When you work for someone else or otherwise don't have a lot of control over your day, you're probably spending a lot of time in the crisis and distractions quadrants. You may be able to have a conversation with your boss about minimizing these or finding ways to head them off better.

When it comes to your time, though, you should be able to stay in the Important and Not Urgent sector. If you're not, either you're not prioritizing correctly, or you're not planning correctly. Either of which encourages distractions and fires that you need to put out.

7. Inspire yourself and track your progress daily.

Never mind the 3%, be in the 1%! That is, those who track their progress to their goal on a daily basis. Did you fall short today? Resolve to do better the next day. If you track as you go along, it's much easier to make adjustments sooner. Otherwise, you might be going down the wrong path for weeks or months and not know it.

This is why your goals have to be measurable. Once

you can measure them, you can figure out how to track them.

Sometimes, this is pretty simple. Suppose you set yourself a goal of writing 500 words a day for five months in order to reach your larger goal of writing a bestseller.

Each day, either you wrote your 500 words or you didn't. Your tracking method could be as simple as putting a big green checkmark on your (paper) calendar each day you write your 500 words. (There are online habit trackers that can help with this as well.)

It's not all about buckling down to the daily tasks. Keep going by making sure you have a source of inspiration each day too. Some people like to use calendars that have different inspirational quotes each day. Others might like to read from a favorite inspirational book or about a favorite inspirational person. Or listen to a podcast, etc.

There are a ton of inspirational sources on the Internet, so find what works for you.

8. Encourage criticism.

We talked about failing and using failure as a lesson

to help us move forward. Criticism can be of assistance in the same way. It's not comfortable, and most of us have been taught from childhood to fear or dread it.

"Criticism may not be agreeable, but it is necessary. It fulfills the same function as pain in the human body. It calls attention to an unhealthy state of things." -Winston Churchill

---

NEVERTHELESS, HOW ELSE WILL YOU IMPROVE? No one person can know everything. Plus, you may have some traits or quirks that come off differently to other people than the way you intend or that you may not even be aware of. Only other people can help you see outside of yourself.

No one becomes better by doing the same thing they've always done. You've got to try something other than what you've been doing. Criticism from other people can help point you in the right direction.

Sure, you might end up talking to people who criticize others just because they can and don't really have anything helpful to say to you, but if you ask for feedback and multiple people tell you the same thing, that's a great way to learn what adjustment you need to make.

Sacrifice Is Necessary

Time is finite, at least for us humans. (Sorry to be the bearer of bad news!) That means it's not possible to do everything you want all of the time and still reach your goals. If you want to be physically fit, you're going to have to give up sleeping in and going to happy hour every day. Same with launching your own business, or becoming a corporate executive, in fact. Certainly, there are industries that still rely on happy hours for networking, but not every night!

"Your level of sacrifice directly determines your level of success." -Anthony Moore

---

It's simple to take the easy way out. The problem is, that doesn't get you to where you want to go. Only discomfort, pain, and yes, failure will help you achieve the success you've been dreaming of.

You can choose your normal life, or you can choose an extraordinary one. Think you can get to extraordinary by doing the ordinary? Of course not. Your peers might be whiling away their evenings on social media. If you want an extraordinary life, you need to be putting in the words in your novel.

Instead of drinking too much at happy hour, build muscle in the gym. Instead of hanging out with your friends at the sports bar, attend a networking event for execs in your field. That is if you're willing to put in the work required and the sacrifices to achieve your goals.

Earlier, we discussed learning to say "no" to ideas that don't serve you. But to be truly successful and live your dream life, you need to take that a step further. Saying "no" to the opportunities that are merely good. This allows you to open up space for the GREAT opportunities.

The time you spend on activities that don't serve you or that are only good opportunities, is time that you can't reclaim. You can't do two things at one time, so you need to pick one. Do you want to focus on the activities that keep you in your normal life, or do you want to choose the ones that lead you to your dreams? The great opportunities, not the good or the mediocre ones?

It's your choice. As the monk says in the movie *Indiana Jones and the Last Crusade*, "Choose wisely."

CHAPTER SUMMARY

- Only 3% of Americans write down their goals, and many of them are afraid of failure and rejection.
- Writing goals down is important for success.
- Rewrite them daily to keep them in mind.
- Set SMART goals: Specific, Measurable, Achievable, Relevant, Time-bound.
- Support your goal efforts with your environment.
- Make lists.
- Minimize distractions and clutter.
- Make the most of mornings and weekends.
- Act 'as if.'
- Find help.
- Manage your time wisely.
- Inspire & track daily.

- Encourage criticism.
- Enormous success requires enormous sacrifice.

IN THE NEXT CHAPTER, WE'LL DISCUSS CREATING routines and, more importantly, sticking to them!

HABIT 4 - CREATING A ROUTINE AND STICKING TO IT

One of the best ways to be successful and achieve your goals is to make it as effortless for yourself as possible. You will need to make sacrifices, as discussed in Chapter 3, and work hard. It's easy to succumb to temptation when you're short on willpower because you had too many difficult decisions to make during the day.

Making your path to success uncomplicated lies in creating daily routines.

Rather than constantly trying to decide each day whether you're going to exercise, how you're going to find time to be inspired, what you're going to eat, when you're going to sleep, and when you'll wake up the next day, create a routine that incorporates these good habits.

No, you probably won't be able to immediately do everything correctly or even right away. It's a process. But, as they say, a journey of a thousand miles starts with one step.

THE IMPORTANCE OF A DAILY ROUTINE

The accumulation of all of your habits is what constitutes a routine. If you have a lot of bad habits or habits that don't move you toward success, your daily routine isn't going to get you to where you want to be.

A good daily routine is a collection of habits that supports your willpower and your journey. Practicing these habits every day removes some of those daily decisions, which helps you to maintain self-control in the face of short-term temptations. Some of these habits may also be directly related to your goals.

For example, if you want to be able to run a marathon in nine months, a daily habit of exercise is a step in the right direction.

There's no question of will you or won't you exercise today. It's the thing you do after drinking your morning glass of water, or what you do on your lunch break, or what you do right after work. Whenever it is that exercise works best for you.

Routines can also save you time. If you typically drop your keys in a particular box near your door, you don't waste time in the morning trying to find them.

When you set out your gym bag the night before, you're not scrambling to get everything in the bag early in the morning, then arriving at the gym only to find you forgot your shoes.

If you think about it, saving just 10 minutes a day saves 60 hours in a given year! Can you think of anything you could use your 60 hours instead of wasting time? Inspiration, fun, time with family, or time spent outdoors?

SETTING UP YOUR NEW AND IMPROVED ROUTINE

Sounds good, but how can you implement a new daily routine, especially if you've got a number of habits that you know you need to replace? It's very hard to break habits and much easier to replace them with something that serves you.

Implement one small change to your routine at a time. Try to match it to your overall goal if you can. Whether you want to lose weight, build muscle, run a marathon, lower your blood sugar, or anything else health-related, exercise is a great place to start. Maybe you're not exercising at all, or you're only exercising once in a while. Wherever you are, begin there. Visit your doctor to make sure you're able to set up an exercise program that won't harm or injure you first.

You'll need to figure out when you can exercise. Depending on your schedule, morning may not be the best time for you. When you exercise in the morning, you know that whatever happens during your day, you won't be thrown off, so it's ideal for many beginners. Commit to setting aside that time whenever it is.

Remember to make it as easy as you can! If you haven't worked out in a while, going hard in the gym to start with is more likely to get you injured. When you haven't been running for a while, trying to jog nine miles is only going to end in frustration and burnout. Walk for ten minutes to begin with. Then you can gradually increase your time.

REPLACING BAD HABITS

You now have the knowledge to implement good habits, but what about bad habits that you don't want anymore? You can't break them because habits are actually hardwired into our brains. Instead, you can replace them with better activities that will help you on the path to achieving your goals. Fortunately, science can tell us how to do this.

All habits are based on three components to make a loop. Cue, routine, and reward. The cue is what triggers the routine, which is the activity or habit that you're doing. It can be positive or negative. If the routine is a healthy exercise, that's great; if it's eating a pint of ice cream after you get home from work, not so much. The final part of the loop is the reward. There's always a reward because that's how your brain sticks to the habit. It's the dopamine release where your brain says; I like it! Let's do more!

These components are there, whether it's a habit that you want to stick to or a habit that doesn't serve you. Maybe you have a habit of reading biographies of inspirational people at night after you wash your dishes. The cue is the dishwashing, which tells you it's now time to read the bio. After you've spent the time reading, your reward is feeling positive and uplifted. A good habit; stick to it.

Or, maybe you have a habit of hitting the cookie jar every time you feel stressed. It could be when your boss yells at you, your spouse yells at you, or someone at the PTA has given you yet another task to complete. The cue is feeling stressed, the activity is eating cookies, and the reward is that feeling you have from eating them. Maybe you feel less stressed for a few minutes or numb. However, even if you're not trying to lose weight, the cookies are harming your body, so that's a habit you want to replace.

Stress and boredom are the most common triggers of bad habits.[1] In order to replace a bad habit, you need to identify what the habit loop is. What is the cue? You know what the habit is that you want to replace. What is the reward you get from the bad habit? You need to acknowledge that there is a reward, even if you don't want to carry out that activity anymore. Understand what it is, because that's part of the power you'll need to replace it and stick to the new one. In addition, identify what the bad habit is doing to you in negative terms so that you can help motivate yourself to stick to the replacement for the bad habit.

That's the first step: figuring out the cue. What are the emotions and circumstances that surround this habit? Suppose you want to stop spending two hours in the evening scrolling through social media.

What's the cue? Maybe you're bored after dinner, you want to escape what happened during the day, or you want some mindless entertainment. Consider what emotion is driving you to sit down in front of a screen (where many people spend their workday anyway). The reward is that you spend a couple of hours being entertained. Plus, every time someone likes a post of yours, you get a quick dopamine hit.

One thing you should know about social media platforms and video games is that they're specifically designed for manufacturing pleasure chemicals in your brain.[2] That keeps you on the platform longer, which allows their advertisers to get more commercials in front of your eyeballs. Even if you don't think you spend too much time on social media, bear that in mind.

The problem with your mindless scrolling and the

reason you want to replace this habit is that you're wasting two precious hours of your day. Time you could be using for something that supports you or actively contributes to your success. In addition, studies show that social media makes most people more depressed.[3]

The next step is to figure out the alternatives—the good or positive activities you can put in place. In this case, a good nighttime habit is reading or listening to inspirational or educational podcasts. You may be trying to acquire more knowledge in your field in order to be promoted, or maybe you're considering a career change, so you need to learn a new skill. Or maybe you haven't yet figured out where to carve out time for your inspirational and motivational reading and/or listening.

This is also a good place to spend quality time with your family. Place all the phones in a separate room, so you can really be with each other.

What's the reward? It depends on the alternative you choose, though certainly knowing that you're setting yourself more firmly on the path to success can help keep you going! Additional rewards may be the joy of learning, or the feeling of inspiration, or increased motivation, or the happiness that comes with connecting with your family.

The third step in your habit replacement is to commit to making these changes and adjusting as you go. A replacement that looks great on paper might not work for you as well as you want it to. You may need to swap in the new, positive activity first and commit to giving it some time before you write it off. You're experimenting! If one doesn't work, that's okay. You'll just need to swap in something else and see if that works.

Finally, plan for failure. Yes, you're going to encounter some bumps in the road, and you will probably not be able to stick to this new good habit right away. Ask yourself ahead of time how you'll deal with it. After all, when you dent your car, do you then go and smash it up entirely? Don't allow it to derail you, but accept it as a temporary setback and keep moving forward.

Plan ahead for stressful times or situations you know are coming up that might test you. What will you do if your boss yells at you at work or if you're under another stressful situation? If your habit is to replace scrolling with spending time with your spouse, what will you do when they're out of town for work?

STICK TO YOUR NEW ROUTINE

With all habits, start small, with something you can actually do right now. If you try to take steps that are too big, you're more likely to get frustrated and stop. Think of it as good table manners. You take a small bite and digest, then another.

Small steps help you stay committed to your routine. Take it easy at first, and build up over time. Using big leaps to get you where you want to go may seem logical, but it actually doesn't work. Life isn't a race, and the story of the tortoise and the hare works for implementing a new daily routine too. The hare leaped ahead fast at first but ended up losing to the tortoise, who was taking small, slow steps, but he kept moving ahead. He didn't get distracted or stop along the way and kept going slowly forward.

Once you've got your new routine in place, you'll be able to move faster on your path to success.

It's too hard to stick to new habits when you're trying to do too many at once. It drains your willpower when the whole point of a routine is to support it instead. Make sure you've cemented one habit into place before starting a new one. That's less of a drain on your self-control.

You don't get from zero to hero in one leap, as fun as that might be. Popular entertainment makes it seem possible, but it doesn't work like that in real life. The successful people who serve as your inspiration didn't suddenly wake up and achieve their goals one day. (Even if it seems like it!) They put in the hard work and sacrifices to get there over time. Just because you didn't see the work they put in doesn't mean it didn't happen.

Good Habits You Should Incorporate

Food, exercise, and sleep are key to your success. We'll discuss food in more detail in Chapter 6 and sleep in a later section in this chapter. In addition to these three, which support your physical and mental health, there are others that will help you to stay focused on your journey.

1. Map it out.

Sometimes, it works better if you work backward

from your goals. Then, you can consider the secondary goals that will help you reach your overall goal. Once you know what you need to do to achieve success, you can map out what you need to do to get there.

For example, suppose you want to write a best-selling book. What's necessary to reach that goal? Writing a book and building a platform that gets people excited about reading (and therefore buying) your book.

Let's look at what you need to write the book. It may be a set number of words per day for a certain number of months. What do you need to be able to write that number of words per day? If you're currently working full time, you may need to carve out time before you go to work, which means rising earlier.

Mapping it out also works when you are beginning your day. What do you need to achieve that day? You probably have tasks at your job that must be completed. How and when will you get them done?

2. Plan for success the night before.

As mentioned before, mornings or the hours after you wake are the most productive. No one's interrupted you yet, and your mind is fresh from its nightly rest.

Does this sound like a good time to be doing things like figuring out what to wear, packing your gym bag, trying to find your keys, or deciding what you're going to have for lunch or breakfast that day?

All those things are much better done the night before. Make the decisions at the end of the day. The next morning you have self-control and willpower available to tackle the difficult decisions for the day. Layout what you need, pack your gym bag, make your lunch in the evening. In the morning, you'll be able to grab and go.

Spend your willpower on the things that matter in your life. Don't fritter it away on little decisions that don't have a big effect on your success.

The evening before you go to bed is also a great time to journal or take notes on what you want to accomplish the next day. The act of writing these ideas down means that your brain doesn't have to waste space on trying to remember them for the next day. It's also a good exercise to note what went well each day and what you might have done differently in retrospect.

When thinking about what didn't go well, don't blame yourself or play "shoulda, woulda, coulda" to make you feel bad. You encountered a situation, and maybe you didn't like how you handled it, or the result didn't come out the way you wanted. You can learn from it for the next time something similar happens. Remember, mistakes are a feature, not a bug!

Noting what you would like to accomplish the next day is also a great way to end your workday. Just as it does when you're at home, this frees your brain up to think about other things. It can also help you make sure that you leave work at work. It's a signal that you're done for the day.

Not only that, now you have your plan for the next day! You won't have to worry about spending time in the morning deciding what you need to tackle. It's already there. You may take the morning to prioritize your tasks for the day.

3. Make your bed.

When you think of an organized, productive person, what do you think they do with their bed in the morning? Leave everything all messed up? Or do they make their beds?

Right. It's another signal to your brain that you are the type of person who makes their bed—an organized, productive person. It can also be a soothing or meditative exercise if you pay attention to it as you're doing it. It gives you a calm and organized way to start the day.

4. Eat breakfast.

You've probably heard this advice before, and it may or may not have made any sense to you. There is a good, scientific reason to eat breakfast—it's not just an urban legend! Eating breakfast tells your body that calories are coming, so it revs up your metabolism.[4]

A healthy breakfast provides more good nutrients and reduces the chance that you'll eat poorly or binge on junk food during the rest of the day. In Chapter 6, we'll discuss what constitutes healthy food, but for now, just know that breakfast sets you up for success for the rest of the day.

5. Do hard work in the morning.

With all the prep work you've done to increase your willpower reserves for the day, leverage them the best you can by tackling the hardest, most important work in the morning. Although you may have to use some of your reserves up to get through the difficult tasks, they won't take up as much as they would later in the day when you're starting to drain away more of your self-control.

Plus, even if the rest of the day devolves into meetings and emails and you get to absolutely nothing else, you'll know you have accomplished a significant task. That's a big boost not only to your motivation but also to your journey to success.

"Eat a live frog first thing in the morning, and nothing worse will happen to you for the rest of the day." -Mark Twain

---

The critical tasks can be thought of like a frog. Eat them at the beginning of the day, and you're well on your way.

6. Clean up after yourself at work and at home.

Even spending just a few minutes at the end of the day at work tidying up your space means that you'll come in the morning ready to eat your frog. You won't need to spend time decluttering and removing the distractions of the previous day.

Wash your dishes after eating (or load them into the dishwasher). There's less chance of vermin that way, and it also closes the loop for your brain. The food is eaten, and the plates are cleared away. That signals to your brain that the meal is over.

In addition, it prevents distraction. If you've decided that you need to get up early to work on your goals, dirty dishes in the sink are extremely unmotivating. Plus, you might be so disgusted by the look of them that you decide they must be taken care of before you can get started on your morning routine, thus squandering your golden opportunity to be productive after waking up.

Spending ten minutes at night cleaning up a room means less time you need to spend doing a big clean-up on the weekend. In the previous chapter, we talked about using your weekends smartly. Cleaning, while necessary, isn't usually the best use of your time.

Cleaning and tidying don't require a lot of brain-power or willpower. Don't waste productive time on them if you can help it. At night, or right after a meal, is a great time to prevent these issues from building up to unmanageable proportions and distracting you from the work you need to be doing.

7. Read and/or listen to inspirational podcasts or other material.

This is a great way to teach yourself new skills and to encourage your movement forward on your path. Most people complain they don't have enough time to read, although this is usually remedied by reducing the time they are spending in front of one screen or another.

Making sure that reading is a part of your daily routine solves that problem!

As you know, it's very easy to fall victim to daily temptations or allow your grand vision to be smothered by unimportant little tasks or to lose confidence in yourself once you encounter an obstacle. Daily motivational and educational reading and listening help keep you focused on the path in front of you.

Also, when you're feeling particularly unmotivated or not confident, reading about others who've had the same or similar issues can help you get over that hump. Renew your self-confidence. If other people can do it, why not you?

．．．

To Sleep, Perchance to Be More Productive

Getting enough sleep is so important that we gave it its own section! You may be thinking, "Well, if I have only twenty-four hours in a day, why should I spend seven to eight hours of it sleeping? Shouldn't I reduce sleep to get more done?" Some people claim they can get by on significantly less, say, four to six hours.

How many cups of coffee do you drink a day? How many energy drinks do you consume? How much caffeine do you need to get through the day? If the answer is more than zero, you're probably not getting enough sleep. Coffee and caffeinated tea do have some beneficial properties, so even if you do get enough sleep, you might choose to drink these anyway. However, if you can't get through the day without it, you probably need to recalibrate the amount of sleep you get.

You may not be able to get to sleep easily, or you may wake up a lot. Too much caffeine can have both of these effects. So can stress. Sleep quality is key to being productive, but why is that?

Here's what happens while you sleep. Since you're not conscious, you may not be aware that very important body functions occur when your conscious mind is at rest. Though popular culture makes it seem like our brains are separate from our bodies, they're not. They're very tightly intertwined (you even have neurons in your gut). There's a lot going on while we sleep.

Some of them are brain-oriented. It helps us form memories, and we appear to incorporate knowledge learned during the day. This is why people tell you to "sleep on it," and after a refreshing night's sleep, you often find that you've solved the problem. The brain also releases some important hormones, such as those responsible for appetite and growth during sleep,[5] but the body also benefits from sleep. Muscle growth and repair, for example, occur at this time.

A study of Chinese adults demonstrated that those who got at least seven hours of sleep reported feeling happy, and those who got less than six were unhappy.[6] Other studies show that adults who get six or fewer hours have a higher mortality rate than those who receive seven to nine.[7]

Now you can see why there are significant consequences to not getting enough sleep. Short-term consequences include lack of memory, a bad mood, and an increased risk of accidents or injury, including on the job. Long-term effects can be even worse, including cardiovascular disease and obesity.[8]

Even though people like to brag about how little sleep they get, they're ignoring the poor performance they're actually putting in. In fact, they may be too sleep-deprived to know how bad their performance actually is! But their boss and coworkers notice.

If you want to be successful and you shirk sleep, you're actually making it harder on yourself and making success less likely. You're making poor decisions, both in the long-term and in the short-term.

Better Sleep Hygiene

There are a number of ways that you can make it easier to fall asleep. Writing down what has happened during the day and what needs to happen the next day, as discussed above, are part of the answer. Here are some more ways to obtain good-quality sleep.

1. Wake and go to bed at the same time each day.

You can't "catch up" on sleep you missed during the

week on the weekend. Unfortunately, it just doesn't work that way. Having a time that you go to sleep and wake up helps your body to understand that now is the time to go to sleep and release melatonin.

You may even find that once you are in a predictable routine, you won't need an alarm clock because you'll end up waking at the time you need to wake up. If you're beginning to wake up earlier in order to get a head start on the day, that will probably take a while! Use an alarm when you need to.

When should you go to bed? Work backward. Suppose you're a seven-hour sleeper, as I am. If you need to wake up at 5 A.M. to begin your day, then you need to go to bed seven hours before that, or 10 P.M.. If you need eight or nine hours, that's 9 or 8 P.M..

Right now, that may seem very early to you! None-theless, how much productive work do you really get done after 7 P.M.? Maybe you send some emails. Anything sent after 7 P.M. is not going to bring you the success you're dreaming of! Are you scrolling through social media at 8 P.M.? You're way better off sleeping or preparing for sleep.

. . .

2. WATCH CAFFEINE AND EXERCISE RIGHT BEFORE bedtime.

Some people are slow metabolizers of caffeine and need to stop ingesting it around 2 P.M. (!). Others can go later. Very strenuous exercise right before bed will leave your heart rate too elevated to sleep comfortably.

The same is true for heavy meals or a lot of alcohol. Your body needs time to digest and process, and sleep is much more difficult if your stomach is still trying to make work of the burger and fries you downed an hour before bedtime.

3. Shut down screens at least an hour before bed.

We moderns have become so tethered to our devices that this may seem inconceivable. But again, what productive work are you doing on your phone at 9 P.M.? Or even 8 P.M.? Emails? Texting? Social media? If you want to connect with your friends, you could always try calling them.

The reason this is such an issue is that our devices emit a certain frequency of blue light, which makes our bodies think it's daytime, so they don't produce the melatonin that's necessary for sleep.[9]

Reading is a great choice for when it's time to put down the devices. You could go old-school with a hardback or paperback, although E-readers don't emit the same blue light as other devices, making them safe for this time too.

4. KEEP SCREENS OUT OF THE BEDROOM.

The best way to produce good sleep quality is to save the bedroom for two things and two things only. Sleep and sex. That's it.

Don't use your phone as an alarm. You can buy extremely cheap alarm clocks that will do the job. Charge your phone in a different room. In addition to helping you sleep better, it also helps prevent squandering the productive time after you wake up. You won't be tempted to check your social media feed or your email. You'll get up and do whatever your morning routine is that it helps you to achieve your goals.

5. Darken the bedroom.

Excessive light often interferes with sleep. Buy blackout curtains. Have you ever been to Las Vegas? Then you know they have curtains that block out even the tiniest bit of outside light. You can rollover, look at the clock, and have absolutely no idea whether it's 3 P.M. or 3 A.M..

If you can't get blackout curtains, get a sleep mask. That works too.

6 Avoid (or cloak) outside noises.

Depending on where you live, you may have a lot of noise outside your bedroom at night. If it's white noise (like traffic rushing by), you may be able to just get used to it.

If not, you can buy a sound generator. They can generate white noise so you can't hear what's going on outside. Or, you might prefer one that produces sounds like rain or ocean waves.

In addition, there are some heavy-duty earplugs out there for you to try.

Whatever issue you may be having with your sleep environment, there is a range of ways that you can improve it. Being mindful of what's keeping you awake can help you figure out what you need to change. For many people, it's as simple as shutting down the devices before bed and keeping them out of the bedroom. Find out what works for you so you can get good-quality sleep that you need for success.

Chapter Summary

- A daily routine can help support your dreams.
- All habits are a loop of cue, activity, and reward. You don't break bad habits so much as replace them.
- Find the milestones of the loop you want to change.
- Decide which alternatives you want to use.
- Commit to using the alternative.
- Adjust and tweak as you go along.
- Food, sleep, and exercise are necessary for good daily habits. There are additional ways to make good daily routines.
- Map it out.
- Plan for success the night before.
- In the morning, make your bed and eat breakfast.
- Tackle your hardest task in the morning ("eat the frog").
- Clean up each day.

- Read and/or listen to educational/motivational content.
- Sleep is important, and most people need seven to nine hours. You also need good-quality sleep.
- Set sleep/wake times.
- Watch caffeine and activity right before bed.
- Shut down screens an hour before bedtime.
- Only sleep and have sex in the bedroom.
- Adjust the bedroom for darkness and silence.

IN THE NEXT CHAPTER, YOU WILL LEARN ABOUT TRULY listening to others instead of reacting.

*W*hat are most of us thinking about when we're in a conversation with other people? What we're going to say next! However, that means that we're not truly listening to what the other person is saying. What if the other person has something valuable to say? We're missing it.

In earlier chapters, we discussed the importance of having a mentor or someone who's either been through what you've been through or has achieved the kind of success that you're seeking. What's the point of finding such a person if you aren't going to hear what they have to say?

We also talked about encouraging criticism earlier

and how it helps you to grow. An objective person can see where they've been making mistakes if they're not already aware of them. Learning what you're doing wrong—and more importantly, figuring out how to fix the errors—is a key step on your path to your goals. People can be so caught up in an argument that they let the comments that would otherwise help them improve slide on by.

ARGUMENTS DON'T SERVE YOU

Even if you think you've won a point, the other person is probably still convinced they're right!

"You can't win an argument. You can't because if you lose it, you lose it, and if you win it, you lose it." -Dale Carnegie

---

Think about the last argument you lost. Did you feel better about yourself? Did you come away convinced that the other person was right? Was your opinion about the matter changed because you saw the sense in what the other person said?

Probably not. More likely, you still felt that you were right or that you had the correct opinion. The other person might have been louder (or quieter), but you felt they won just because they had better debate training than you did or some other reason unrelated to the content of what they said. You probably kept arguing mentally, and minutes or hours later, you came up with the perfect comeback, what you should have said to counter them.

Your mind, however, remained unchanged. Do you think it's any different when you're on the winning side of an argument? Looking back, do you think any of the people you argued with changed their minds because of the content of what you had to say? It's unlikely.

Whether you win or lose, you haven't really made anyone reconsider their position. You've likely done no more than making the other person feel bad about you, themselves, or both. That's not going to assist you in your quest.

Understanding Why Arguments Don't Work

As human beings, we evolved to have special areas of the brain that other animals don't have (the prefrontal cortex, among others). Yet, we still have the animal brain as well. You may have heard it referred to as the "lizard" or "reptilian" brain. This is where our fight-or-flight instinct comes from, and it makes decisions very quickly. It uses shortcuts and rules of thumb because those help us to make faster choices.

Why is this so important? It's how we survived as a species. When we were on the savannah, if we stood around and thought about what we should do when we spotted a tiger in the grass, we'd get eaten. We needed to be able to run when we saw the danger.

We're pattern-seeking animals. This also helped us to survive. If we associate the waving of a field of grass with a tiger being in it, then we are more likely to avoid being eaten. Whereas if we didn't, and the tiger was there, we would be eaten. There wasn't much consequence of being wrong about seeing the pattern if there actually wasn't one but a very severe one if we ignored an actual pattern.

On top of this simple brain that we share with other animals, we evolved a more complex one that helps us make deliberate decisions and led to language, algebra, and smartphones. This part of the brain takes longer to mature (it isn't "ripe" until we're in our early twenties), and it takes up a lot of energy. This is where willpower comes from.

You don't see your family dog deciding whether or not to eat a treat. He'll just wolf it down. Does your cat think about whether it needs exercise if it sees a mouse running across the floor? Its predator instincts cause the chase. Animals don't have a human brain, and they have no use for willpower or self-control.

Human brains prefer to be efficient, so they'd rather use the fast, shortcut system rather than slow down and use their deliberative power. In other words, the lizard brain is the default. Because of the way we evolved, there are certain cognitive biases that we're all subject to, which makes our brains faster.

A big one is that humans like to be right. If you've ever had a pet cat, you know they'll stare straight at you while they do something like knocking a glass of water on the floor. They have no concept of right or wrong, but we do. Our desire to be right comes along with confirmation bias, where we notice the evidence that supports our thought or opinion and ignores anything that conflicts with it.

What happens when we encounter evidence that we're wrong?

Our brains really don't like it. It can accept that we're wrong, or it can negate the new evidence in some way so that we can keep believing we're right. Guess which one happens! Hint: it's not the acceptance of being wrong.

When someone comes to you and tells you that you're wrong, what do you do? Agree that you're wrong? No, you try to pick apart what they're saying, or you might dismiss them as not knowing what they're talking about. You might concentrate on one part of their argument, which (you believe) is clearly wrong and ignore the larger point.

In other words, we're pretty much wired to learn absolutely nothing from arguments.

When You Need to Persuade Others

Although you may need to listen more to your mentors than to convince them of something, there are times when you want to sway someone over to your side. Maybe you're up for the big promotion, and you want your boss to agree to it. You want an agent who's handled bestselling books similar to yours to handle the book you've just written.

Now, you know arguing with them isn't going to yield results and can, in fact, make you worse off. What can you do instead? Obviously, baldly telling them that they're wrong is not the way to go. Instead, show that you respect their opinions.

Admit that you could be wrong. That immediately helps them put their guard down and think that maybe they could be wrong too. This way, you're heading off their need to be right. If you don't have to be right, they don't have to defend themselves against being wrong. Can you see how that immediately puts someone in a better headspace?

It also puts you in the right mindset. Now you don't have to defend or criticize either. You're just trying to get to the truth of the matter. You can ask questions to get them thinking about why you might be right. These questions can also help you understand their perspective better.

Respecting someone else's opinion requires that you allow them to express their opinion. No interruptions, even if you're sure that you know what they'll say next. You might be surprised! You can practice this in daily conversations, listening without interrupting. It doesn't have to be anyone special or in a position of authority; you could practice listening to your colleague telling you about the funny thing his dog did yesterday. Be mindful and present as you listen.

Demonstrate That You're Listening and Paying Attention

In order to be honest and real in a conversation, people need to feel comfortable with the person they're speaking with. They don't want to feel defensive or angry. They want to think that they will be able to express themselves openly without being misunderstood or have their opinions taken the wrong way and out of context.

Whew! It sounds like a tall order! However, as a listener, you can show the person speaking that you are open to what they have to say. You are interested, not interesting. No one wants to "spill their guts" if they think they'll be interrupted or that their listener only wants to one-up them. Fortunately, there are nonverbal ways in which you can express your intent to listen and understand.

The following methods demonstrate to the person you're listening to that you want to hear them. They'll see that you find them important enough to listen to, which immediately helps you build trust together. Everyone's favorite topic is themselves!

"Talk to someone about themselves, and they'll listen for hours." -Dale Carnegie

---

1. Face them directly.

Whether you're standing or sitting, make sure that you are looking directly at them. Not at your watch or the door or the rest of the room to see if someone cooler is around to talk to.

That probably seems pretty obvious, but what about your feet if you're standing? They should also point directly at the person you're talking to. Not at the door, the brunch bar, or at the cute guy or girl standing three feet away. Your whole body should be open to the person you're listening to.

This stance tells them that they're interesting, and so they have your full attention.

Make sure you're on the same level as they are. If they're sitting and you're standing, you've left them in a more vulnerable position. This also makes you look authoritarian. When you're trying to get to know someone or hear the great things they have to say, you don't want to seem like a dictator.

2. Put down the phone.

This skill is something you'll probably need to practice. When you're listening to someone, you do not need to be on your phone. We discussed minimizing distractions earlier in the book. Your phone is a distraction, particularly when you're trying to build relationships.

Imagine your life after you've reached your goals. You've put all the habits in this book into place, and as a result, you're incredibly successful. You're at the point where you're now the mentor, talking to younger people about everything you did to reach your goals.

A young person approaches you, seeming eager to learn from you. They tell you that they've long admired you from afar and that you're their role-model. They ask you a question related to your success. Just as you're about to answer it, they whip out their phone, immediately breaking eye contact and paying no attention to you whatsoever. Then they put the phone back in their pocket and ask you the question again.

How do you think you'd feel if that happened to you? Insulted, probably. How important can they possibly think you are if they break off the conversation to look at their phone? More importantly, do you have any desire to mentor this youngster? You might even have walked off when they pulled out their phone!

That's exactly how the person you're supposed to be listening to feels when you take out your phone. If you're waiting on an urgent call, maybe now is not the time to approach someone else. If there's nothing urgent, your phone is going to prevent you from building a relationship. Not make it stronger.

3. Relax your hands and arms.

What do you think when you see someone clenching their fists? Probably that they're angry or upset. Do you want to go over and talk to them? No, you'd rather wait until they simmer down and relax.

It's the same when you're listening to someone else. If they see you clenching your fists, they have no way of knowing that you're angry about something that happened earlier in the day or that clenching your fists is a nervous habit. All they know is that you appear angry when they're speaking.

Sometimes, you might just be tense because you're in a setting you're not used to. For example, many people get nervous at networking events. It's perfectly natural, but if your hands and arms are tense, it's not clear to others that you're nervous about the event. It doesn't put the speaker at ease. Consciously relax them.

4. Avoid defensive positions.

No one wins an argument, and most people don't really want to get into one anyway. When you look defensive, it appears that you might start one. These positions also suggest that you've stopped listening because you heard something you didn't like. It causes the people around you to be uncomfortable.

A common example is crossing your arms in front of your chest. Now, you might just be cold. If so, put on a sweater or a jacket. The person you're listening to has no way of knowing that you're cold.

Another one is shielding yourself with an item held in front of your chest, like a file folder or purse. This makes you look anxious, which causes your speaker to become uncomfortable.

5. Maintain eye contact.

You don't want to be creepy, but people feel heard and understood when you're making a good amount of eye contact.

Don't stare at the floor, your hands, their hands, the door, or the cutie standing three feet away. Signal that you are interested in the speaker with your eye contact.

6. Smile.

Believe it or not, this is one of the best ways to establish trust with another person. It shows that you're interested and friendly towards them, which makes people more likely to feel interested in you and friendly in return.

These ways of showing interest can be practiced pretty much at any time with anyone. You can rehearse these with colleagues, friends, relatives, and the owner of the corner market. Plant your feet and stand relaxed when you're having a conversation. Make sure you're making eye contact when the other person speaks and relax your hands. Practice can be especially effective when you run into your boss (or their boss) in the elevator or cafe at work.

UNDERSTAND THE OTHER PERSON'S POINT OF VIEW

The path to success includes people skills. Being able to see things from another person's perspective is what makes successful relationships. Not only with your spouse or significant other, but with your supervisor (and their supervisor), clients, colleagues, mentors, and friends.

Building these types of relationships starts when you're thinking of others. In conversation, you're not just trying to figure out what you're going to say next. You're curious about what they have to say because you want to get to know them. You already know you, and the next step is to learn about others.

You don't have to worry about your own personality when you're trying to get to know someone else. It's better to be interested (in them) than interesting. Curiosity takes you a long way when you're trying to see the world from another's point of view.

Knowing yourself is still important, however. It can help you regulate your emotions and stay in control if the other person unwittingly triggers something that's an issue for you. When you're in a conversation, it's not about you. Refocus on what the other person is saying. Yes, there may be times when someone's being malicious and trying to push your buttons, but you probably know who those people are.

If you're talking to someone who doesn't know you well, how could they know they're aggravating you? They can't. They obviously meant nothing by it, and the problem is you and your reaction to it, not them. Get back to the conversation and what the other person is trying to convey to you.

Being empathetic creates a strong interpersonal space between the two of you. It's not about seeing the situation from your point of view or the particular tack you would take in a given situation. How might the other person react? Try to understand why they're doing what they're doing. It may not be what you would do, but that doesn't make it wrong.

Our emotions can help us read the other person better. They might be saying words that we want to hear or what they think we want to hear, but do their emotions match what they're saying? Do they feel uncomfortable talking to you? Helping someone else get comfortable with you is a great way to gain perspective on them.

Are you interpreting what they say correctly? Some people aren't very good at expressing themselves, while others are quite verbal. It's easy for misunderstandings to arise because you have your experience, and they have theirs. If you don't think you're getting it right, make sure you ask questions to ensure that you're not misinterpreting.

Different experiences also lead to different opinions and ways of looking at the world. Remember, this isn't an argument. You're trying to communicate and persuade, so you need to be open to the fact that there will be differences between you. That doesn't mean one of you is right, and one of you is wrong. Remember to respect their opinion.

You'll get to know people much more easily when you respect what they have to say. They'll be more open with you, and you can benefit from their knowledge and experience. Even if you're trying to persuade them to do something you want them to do.

It's also helpful if you can get to know someone when you want to sway them over to your side. If you have an idea of things they don't like to hear, you can try to avoid them when you're making your suggestions. You don't have to change your personality like a chameleon to fit into every group you're in, but it does help to have an awareness of the likes and dislikes of the people you're speaking to.

For example, your boss might hate complaints. She wants you to suggest solutions to the problems you're having instead of just coming to her venting about whatever your issue is. If you want her to support your promotion, don't complain! Even if you want to. Every time you have a problem, come to her with a suggestion for how to make it better.

And here's a hint for you: no one wants to hear your complaints! Come up with a solution before you approach anyone with a problem. In this way, you're respecting their need for effective use of their time and energy.

Avoiding Common Mistakes When Viewing From Another's Perspective

As much as we've discussed, there is no right or wrong answer, only two different perspectives.

People can get caught up in empathizing and actually detract from success. How is this possible?

The first mistake is not truly understanding the other's perspective while thinking that you have. Especially if you have genuinely tried to see the world from someone else's viewpoint. You may pat yourself on the back for a job well done, when in fact, you didn't get it at all. Unfortunately for you, studies have shown that people are bad at reading others and overconfident in their own accuracy.[1]

If you think you understand, check-in. You can say something like, "I'm hearing you say..." and then whatever it is, you thought you understood. If you got it wrong, they'll tell you! This way, there are no hard feelings due to misinterpretations on either side. You want the other person to know that you're doing your best to see the world in the same way that they do and that it's important to you that you get it.

The second mistake is to take the other's perspective as gospel without verifying the underlying assumptions. Maybe the person sees things in a certain way because their facts aren't based on reality. Maybe they're relying on hearsay or evidence they have not verified for themselves. (This can

happen to you too, of course!) Reaching an agreement based on faulty facts or assumptions, whether
they're yours or the other person's, won't help
either.

The trick is to understand where they're coming
from first and express it. Then you can find a way to
challenge something that's false if you realize that's
the case. It won't always be the case because people
can disagree with you based on the same facts that
you have in front of you. Don't assume that they're
wrong about something simply because they
disagree with you.

Positive Perspectives

In fact, honestly, seeking out opposing viewpoints
will help you gain perspective. You may find similar-
ities with your own. In fact, you could end up real-
izing that the gap in perspective between you is
actually distinctions without a difference. Or you
may find that the difference is due to different
values from yours, which may be equally valid and
something to consider.

True interaction will help you understand a different
viewpoint better. As noted above, people are actually

not that great at being able to tell whether they got it or not. So ask questions. Get curious and interested.

When you're interested, you'll find it much easier to listen without responding. Your concern will naturally be to make sure that their opinions and thoughts are coming through to you correctly. By contrast, when you're trying to be interesting instead, you're thinking about yourself, your opinions, and thoughts.

Build trust first to ensure that looking at things from another perspective helps you to understand and doesn't drive you apart. If the trust isn't there, different viewpoints will only serve to cement your disagreement.

When you're satisfied that you truly understand the other perspective, then you can be objective about it. Is it based on truth, or are there faulty assumptions? Pull back and look at it from a bird's eye or high-level viewpoint.

Can you work together to find the solution or at least manage the disagreement?

Basing decisions on objectivity—allowing your human, deliberate brain to get involved—means better choices. You might even get to a win-win agreement, where both sides can feel good about what they've done.

Chapter Summary

- No one wins an argument, nor do they learn anything from it.
- Show that you respect others' opinions by listening and not responding unless you need to ask questions. Practice this skill with anyone at work or at home.
- Use nonverbal communication to show that you're listening. These techniques can also be practiced with anyone.
- Face the person directly with your whole body.
- Put your phone away.
- Relax your limbs.
- Avoid defensive postures.
- Maintain eye contact.
- Smile.
- Understand the other's point of view because empathy is the key to success.
- Clarify to make sure you truly understand.

- Take an objective look at the situation once you've got it.
- Find opposing viewpoints to help you better understand.
- Honestly interact with the new viewpoint.

IN THE NEXT CHAPTER, YOU WILL LEARN HOW AND why nutrition is crucial for you to achieve the life you want.

Some readers may intuitively understand why eating right is important for success. Nevertheless, others may be wondering what food has to do with it. So many of the techniques we've discussed so far involve mindset, willpower, and other habits that seem like they have to do with the brain. Not so much the body.

We've already discussed the importance of breakfast and managing blood sugar. What more is there to say? Plenty! Though Western cultures tend to think of the mind and body as being separate entities, they're not. Neurons and other cells in your body provide feedback to the brain, which then releases one chemical or another in response to the signals from the body. Rather than thinking of your brain and body as a duality, recognize instead that they're both integral parts of the organism that is you. This fact will help you to remember the three physical habits of good food, sleep, and exercise as crucial to your success.

FEED YOUR HEAD

Your brain is a resource hog. It's only about 2% of your total weight, but it requires about 20% of your daily energy use just for itself.[1] Most of the unconscious bodily functions are directed by the brain, such as regulating breathing, telling the pancreas to release insulin, sending instructions to the muscles when you want to raise your arm, etc. In addition to the tasks we've discussed earlier in this book, like remembering where you put your keys, deciding whether or not to take the promotion, and taking an objective look at another person's point of view while you're in conversation with them, use executive functions that only appear to happen in humans.

The brain runs entirely on glucose, which you may already know is a form of sugar. Carbohydrates quickly break down into glucose, where protein takes much longer to do so. Without enough glucose, the brain can't function correctly. Protein is primarily used for muscle building and forming other proteins the body needs for various processes. Fats break down into fatty acids that are mostly used for the creation of hormones and for cell linings.

FUEL QUALITY

Back in the 1980s, when personal computing was just starting to get off the ground, programmers liked to throw around the acronym GIGO. It's somewhat fallen out of favor but is just as true today as it was then: Garbage In, Garbage Out.

The same goes for your mind and body. Your brain is not a computer, though pop culture likes to think of it that way. However, it's also true for you: put garbage in and get garbage out. (Not literally!) If you give your brain and body bad quality food, you're not going to get the thinking power out of it that you want, nor will you get the athletic performance you're seeking.

Want to run a marathon? Pizza and candy aren't going to get you through 26.2 miles! Carbohydrates provide a quick hit of glucose, so they're handy when you feel your blood sugar dropping too low, or when you're at mile 20, and you need something to power through those last few miles, but you need protein for a more steady burn so you can go the distance.

It's no different when your goal is more cerebral, like writing a bestseller or reaching the executive level at the company. Bad fuel means your brain won't run at peak performance. That increases the likelihood of making bad decisions. (Sure, you can go to your pal's bachelor party the night before the big presentation! How could that go wrong?)

YOU MIGHT NEED MEDICINE AFTER A FEW Spoonfuls of Sugar

If the brain needs glucose, then eating sugar must be great for you, right? Not so fast! When your body recognizes that you've ingested some glucose, the pancreas releases insulin, which means that your mind and body now recognize that you're metabolizing some food, and your brain lets everything know that you're not hungry. (You've probably heard that it takes about 20 minutes for all the signals to reach each other and your feeling of hunger to subside.)

Fructose is another sugar, but it's not all that great for the body when eaten by itself. Sucrose (table sugar) and HFCS (high-fructose corn syrup) both contain glucose and fructose. The problem with fructose is that it's only metabolized in the liver. Why is that such a problem? Having more calories processed in the liver means that more of the "bad" cholesterol (that causes cardiovascular and other diseases) gets produced, compared with glucose alone. It also produces more fat and some other byproducts like uric acid, which aren't helpful for your body either.

Fructose also makes it harder for your body to recognize that it's consuming calories. You keep eating and eating without being able to tell that you're full. Fructose inhibits the release of a protein called leptin, which is one of the main chemicals involved in feeling full.

Avoid drinking soda—it's nothing but fructose (and salt to make you come back for more!). You don't feel full, and you're ingesting calories that cause nothing but damage. Drink water instead.

Fructose is present in fruit, which is a food most people need to eat more. Why is it okay to eat fruit if it's full of this type of sugar? Because fruit has fiber, so leptin gets released. Fiber is crucial to keep your body humming along, and having waste products get flushed out efficiently.

The fiber present in the fruit is why it's recommended that you eat the fruit and not drink it.

Much of the fiber is squeezed out when the fruit is juiced. True, a glass of orange juice provides you with some vitamins and minerals that are not present in, say, a glass of soda, but you get the fructose problem with juice.

Also, protein has the same effect with fructose. If they're eaten together, the protein will allow the leptin to release. You'll feel full in about twenty minutes. That's why an apple with peanut butter is such a great snack!

INFLAMMATION

What exactly is it? Inflammation is actually part of your body's immune response. When you're injured or infected, chemicals are released to help fight the issue, causing inflammation. Fever is a type of inflammation that shows you're trying to fight something off.

Like stress chemicals such as cortisol, it's okay to experience inflammation from time to time. The problem comes when it's more or less chronic. That's when these chemicals can do some damage instead. Sugar (fructose particularly) causes inflammation. Too much overtime leads to cardiovascular disease, diabetes, etc.

Research shows that sugary drinks and too many refined carbohydrates and sugars lead to heart disease.[2] There's also an increased risk of cancer due to increased and chronic inflammation. In addition, excess sugar has been linked to other illnesses like mental decline, arthritis, and liver disease, such as the nonalcoholic fatty liver.

Avoid the Sugar Habit

In Chapter 4, we talked about the difficulty of breaking habits. Instead, they need to be replaced. Hopefully, by now, you understand the importance of removing sugar from your diet, especially fructose, when it's not in combination with fiber and/or protein. If you eat a lot of sugary foods or drink a lot of sugary drinks, you'll need to replace them. And yes, alcohol is by and large a sugary drink, especially when it's mixed up as a pina colada or a margarita, etc.

1. Eat unprocessed foods.

The easiest way to avoid the damage that sugar does to you is to replace it with unprocessed foods. These are foods closest to their natural state as possible. If you pick anything (tomatoes, nuts, lemons, apples, berries) off its tree or shrub, it's totally unprocessed. If it's in a produce bin at the market and not in a box, a can, or a sealed bag, you're good to go.

Some things like rice, barley, and other grains come in bags and boxes, but they're still unprocessed, as long as they're not flavored or in any kind of "style." Those labels signal processing.

Similarly, your (animal) protein should recognizably look like it came from an animal: an egg, loin chop, sirloin steak, or poultry thigh with the bone attached. If it looks like a nugget, patty, or recognizable geometric shape, you're heading into the processed territory, which doesn't necessarily mean that it should never be eaten, just that you need to look more carefully at the ingredients.

Other forms of protein may come in a bag or a box, but they still might be pretty close to their natural state. For example, you might pick up bags of beans or quinoa that aren't processed, as long as they're not flavored or mixed with anything else.

2. If you're eating processed foods, check the labels for the ingredients.

Food manufacturers put in cheap additives to your processed food and then make you pay for these wholly unnecessary substances, like HFCS. They also know that we're all trying to eat these days healthily, so they splash phrases like "all-natural," "healthy," "non-GMO," or whatever on the packaging when these words have absolutely no meaning whatsoever.

If you're on a specific diet, know that the products marketed to you are usually highly processed. You don't get a cauliflower crust pizza without lots and lots of processing! Don't be fooled by the fact that "cauliflower" is in the name.

All protein bars and granola bars are processed, and most of them have quite a bit of sugar hiding in there one way or another. Don't get taken by marketing if it has a name like "nice" or "peaceful." The name means nothing. Check the ingredients.

What are you looking for? See what the first three

ingredients are. Ingredients are listed in the order in which they're present, so the first ingredient is what the product mostly consists of. If that first ingredient is sugar, you're eating a food that is mostly sugar.

Do the best you can to avoid "foods" that have sugar in one form or another as one of the first three ingredients. You already know to avoid HFCS and table sugar, but also avoid the other sweeteners that masquerade as healthier: brown rice syrup, agave syrup, anything that is a "syrup," and anything that ends in "-ose" like maltose or dextrose, etc..

Also, no need to be misled by people who tell you to avoid "chemicals." Pretty much everything already in your body is a chemical. Water is a chemical. Dihydrogen monoxide sure sounds scary, doesn't it? It's just another way to refer to water, which has two hydrogen atoms and one oxygen atom.

Work on making sure your food is as close to its natural state as possible, and when you need to add in processed food, watch the sugar in it.

3. There's no need for most people to drink diet sodas, sports drinks, and energy drinks.

As shown earlier, sugary drinks don't do anything

for you except cause harm. If you want to achieve success, make it as easy as possible. Don't force yourself to fight inflammation when it's not necessary.

Many people like the fizz of soda or that's what they're used to drinking. The natural replacement for regular soda is diet or light soda, right?

Maybe in terms of taking away the sugar, but if you're looking to reach your goals, diet sodas don't actually help you. They can cause harm as well! Drinking diet soda is associated with the increased risk of cardiovascular disease, brain conditions like dementia and stroke, and others. It's not clear from the data, whether that's directly related to diet drinks or whether those who drink diet soda typically have other health conditions. However, diet drinks do seem to be related to changes in neurotransmitters like dopamine, and the sweet flavors may create cravings for more sweet stuff.[3]

Having said that, using diet soda as a way to reduce the amount of sugary soda you imbibe is a good first step. However, over time you'll need to replace the diet drinks as well.

Sports drinks are heavily marketed and usually

contain some kinds of electrolytes and often sugar as well. I may be stating the obvious, but drinking the same beverage that athletes drink doesn't make you a sports-star!

Most people don't need sports drinks. Weight lifting sessions typically aren't grueling enough that you're sweating enough to replace electrolytes. If you're not working out hard for at least an hour, all you need is water. Walking, jogging, and bicycling at an easy pace for less than an hour does not require anything else.

Those of you who are training for a marathon or a triathlon might find sports drinks pretty useful once you pass the one-hour mark. Save it for then.

Energy drinks are best for the companies that sell them. Hopefully, if you've implemented the sleep hygiene habits in Chapter 4, you have enough energy during the day to take care of all of the tasks you've planned. They typically contain caffeine, as well as other supplements such as taurine, ginseng, and others, including sugar, which is always good for a short burst of energy.

People have had to go to the emergency room after consuming these beverages.[4] Energy drinks make it take longer for the heart chambers to squeeze and relax. This change increases the likelihood of a disturbance in a heartbeat and a sudden heart attack. You're definitely going to find it more difficult to achieve your goals when you're in the ER.

If you're tired, there are safer ways to ingest caffeine.

4. Drink water, tea, and coffee.

The absolute best liquid for human beings is water. We're mostly made of water—60% of our body weight![5]

Water is how we regulate body temperature. When we get too hot, we evaporate some of our water as sweat, which cools off the skin. If this water doesn't get replenished, the body starts losing electrolytes and plasma in the blood.

It's key for our brains too. They need plenty of water in order to function at peak performance. Many times when people are dehydrated, they get headaches. That's the brain crying out for more water. When you don't have enough water in your body, it's hard to focus, and your short-term memory is compromised as well.

Water helps cushion joints, tissues, and the spinal

cord, so you can stay active for longer. Once you're dehydrated, power and performance start declining. For this reason, when you're working out, drink plenty of water.

You also need water to get rid of toxins and excess material. A healthy fluid intake reduces constipation. It also helps your kidneys work more effectively and reduces the chance of kidney stones. Plus, it increases your metabolic rate to provide energy.

Water is also prevalent in the healthy, unprocessed foods discussed above. Fruits and vegetables are high in water content, so they count toward your fluid requirement, yet they are not sufficient. You still need to drink actual water.

If your urine is pale in color, you're doing a good job with hydration! Keep it up. If it's darker than that, drink more water immediately. Severe dehydration leads to things like seizures, kidney failure, and brain swelling.

If you don't like water, it doesn't matter. You still need to drink it. There are a number of things you can do to make it more palatable, though. If you don't like room temperature water, try it iced or hot and see if that makes a difference.

If you're a big fan of the carbonation in soda, try plain seltzer. There are plenty available that have some flavoring but no calories. You can also flavor your plain or sparkling water yourself. Add a slice of lemon, lime, orange, or cucumber.

Make sure you have water with you at all times so that you can take a sip whenever you like. Plastic bottles are extremely bad for the environment, so get a bottle that you can stick in the dishwasher. There are all kinds of materials and designs, so you'll be able to find one that you like.

Hydration is especially important when you fly because of how dry the air in the plane is. You can carry your empty bottle through the security checkpoint and then fill it up once you get through. That way, you also get to save on the overpriced water they sell at the airport!

How much should you be drinking? Guidelines vary. Most recommendations are eight-ounce glasses per day, which is the equivalent of 2 liters or half a gallon. Obviously, if you're going for a long, hot hike or other exercises, you'll need more. Your urine color will tell you if you didn't drink enough.

It is possible to drink too much water, a condition

known as hyponatremia when your kidneys can't get rid of the excess water. This is extremely rare and seen mostly in extreme or endurance athletes. Healthy adults with a regular diet will find it very difficult to make this happen.

Other beverages such as tea and coffee will also help you in your quest for success. Herbal tea, which has no caffeine in it, is essentially the same as flavored water and doesn't add extra calories or sugars to your diet.

Both coffee and tea have demonstrated health benefits (as long as you're not dosing them with sugar and cream.) They contain antioxidants, which have certain protective properties for your body.

Tea (green and black) contains catechins, which have been shown to reduce the risk of heart disease. Drinking green tea is also associated with reduced risk of some cancers.[6] Coffee is linked to a reduced risk of Type 2 diabetes, as well as an antioxidant that dampens inflammation and makes insulin more effective in the body.

Tea has less caffeine than coffee. Too much caffeine can leach calcium from your bones if you're not taking in enough calcium in your daily diet.

If you're feeling the need for a little boost of energy, try tea, coffee, or both. (Although not at the same time.)

FOOD FOR THOUGHT

There are some chemicals and substances that are particularly good for our cells and the structure of the brain and body. They're typically better absorbed through food. Replacing junk and sugary food is more easily done when you find foods that have added benefits.

1. Omega-3 fats

Although the low-fat craze Americans endured about a decade ago, fats are not "bad," they're necessary. Our brain structure is full of fat (60%), and about half of that is comprised of omega-3.[7] This type of fat helps build nerve and brain cells and may help ward off neurodegenerative diseases.

Much of the fat we eat, assuming it's a healthy fat and not some partially hydrogenated franken-fat, is Omega-6. Many of us need to increase the omega-3 balance. It's found in fatty fish like salmon, sardines, and trout. (Eat the sardine bones too for a calcium boost.)

Walnuts also contain omega-3, though not all nuts do.

2. CAFFEINE

Caffeine is even more beneficial than we noted above in the discussion of tea and coffee. It boosts one of your feel-good neurotransmitters, called serotonin, too, and improves concentration. Don't, however, abuse it.

3. Antioxidants (Anthocyanins, Flavonoids, Curcumin)

Why are antioxidants so important for good health? They fight oxidative stress and inflammation. Certain molecules lose an atom when they're stressed, called free radicals. If there are too many free radicals in the bloodstream, they can clump up and cause damage to the heart and other organs.

Antioxidants have a place for the free radical to attach, so they basically scoop up these dangerous atoms to prevent them from doing too much damage.

Anthocyanins are the type of antioxidant found in red, blue, and purple foods like blueberries. All berries are good, and blueberries especially may help brain cells communicate with each other. They improve your memory too.

Flavonoids are present in dark chocolate. They seem to enhance memory and help prevent age-related decline in the brain. The chocolate itself also appears to be a mood-booster. However, milk chocolate has too much sugar and other substances to be of use. Stick to dark chocolate.

Curcumin is one of the few substances that can cross the barrier between the blood and the brain. It's present in turmeric, so eat your curry! Curcumin has been shown to boost mood because it affects both serotonin and dopamine. It may also protect against Alzheimer's and help prevent plaque tangles in the brain that lead to the disease.

4. Vitamins B, C, E, and K

All vitamins are great, of course, which does not mean that too much is better, by the way.

B vitamins (which include folate) are mood boosters, help slow age-related mental decline, make some brain chemicals, and regulate sugar in the brain. That's a tall order! Get your Bs from eggs.

Vitamin C protects the brain from age-related decline, diseases such as Alzheimer's, and cell damage. Citrus fruit is your best Vitamin C bet. You can also find it in red bell peppers, guava fruit, tomatoes, strawberries, and kiwis, which are small but mighty.

Want to shield your brain cell membranes from inflammation and damage? Vitamin E steps up to the plate here. It's found in nuts, which contain other brain benefits as well.

Vitamin K may not be as popular as some of the other vitamins out there. However, it's necessary for forming the kinds of fat that are tightly packed into brain cells. You can find it in high concentrations in broccoli.

5. Copper, iron, magnesium, and zinc

What are all these metals and minerals doing in your brain? It turns out that very small amounts are crucial for brain health too. Copper helps control nerve signals, and if those aren't working right, there's a higher risk of brain diseases.

Zinc is also involved in nerve signaling. Not having enough has been linked to Parkinson's and depression. Iron is necessary for brain function and leads to "brain fog" if you don't get enough.

You need magnesium for learning and memory. Not enough magnesium is associated with depression, epilepsy, and migraines.

You don't need much, and in fact, one food will give you all these nutrients in one small package. Pumpkin seeds! That's right. Pepitas are good for you (unless they're doused in salt and sugar, of course).

6. Choline

This nutrient is key in the production of acetylcholine, a neurotransmitter that helps your brain with mood and memory. Studies show that it's linked to better brain functioning and better memory. Eggs are an excellent source of choline. Your egg-white omelet isn't going to get you there, though. The yolk is where this key ingredient is located, so make sure you're getting enough whole eggs in your diet.

. . .

7. L-theanine

L-theanine another one of the rare nutrients that is capable of passing through the barrier between the blood and the brain. It assists in boosting the neurotransmitter GABA, which helps you feel more relaxed and decreases anxiety. In addition, L-theanine boosts alpha waves, which also help you relax (but without tiring you out).

Green tea is a great source for L-theanine. In addition, its antioxidants, known as polyphenols, help with memory and protect against neurodegenerative diseases.

CHAPTER SUMMARY

- Human brains and bodies are linked in numerous ways, so nutrition is also important when trying to achieve your Big Hairy Audacious Goals (as well as your secondary goals).
- Our brains run on glucose, but too much sugar, particularly fructose, causes physical damage.

- Similar to other habits, the routine of eating sugar can be replaced with healthier choices.
- Eat unprocessed foods as close to their natural state as possible.
- If you need to eat processed foods, make sure sugar is not one of the first three ingredients.
- Most people should avoid diet soda, energy, and sports drinks.
- Drink plenty of water, plus tea and/or coffee for caffeine when you need it.
- Specific nutrients are good for the brain and protect against memory loss, Alzheimer's, and other neurodegenerative diseases. They're found in everyday whole foods.
- Walnuts contain omega-3 fats
- Nuts (including walnuts) are good sources of Vitamin E
- Whole eggs (not the whites) contain choline and B vitamins
- Broccoli is rich in Vitamin K
- Pumpkin seeds contain zinc, iron, copper, and magnesium
- Dark chocolate has flavonoids
- Green tea is rich in L-theanine

- Oranges (and other citrus) are great for Vitamin C
- Curry (turmeric) contains curcumin, and blueberries are rich in anthocyanins
- Caffeine is present in coffee (and black or green tea, but not herbal)

IN THE NEXT CHAPTER, YOU WILL LEARN TO BE comfortable with discomfort so you push yourself hard in the direction of your goals.

HABIT 7 - PUSH YOURSELF HARDER THAN ANYONE ELSE

*I*f you've implemented the other six habits or rungs on the ladder to success, by now, you should be feeling pretty good. You've got some daily routines that don't wear out your willpower before you encounter a tough day at the office. You've got some inspirational reading (or listening) at some point during the day, and you've adjusted your bedroom to get a good night's sleep. You've traded in your sugary soft drinks for water, and you know that success is possible for you personally.

Maybe some of you are ready to take flight, but many may still feel stuck. We have to put that last rung in place, stack the seventh and final habit on top of the rest.

. . .

What Are You Afraid Of?

Fear is a big sticking point for a lot of people. It might be a general problem that you have to work through, or it might be something that only seems to pop up every now and then when the path to achievement suddenly becomes very rough.

It's one of the emotions that can stop you in your tracks. Often, the first thing that comes to mind isn't necessarily, "I'm scared," but rather, "I can't!" As you now know, the fundamental basis for your success is believing that you can do it. Spending too long on "I can't" means you run the risk of not being able to get going again. Friction has brought you to a stop, and you're no longer in motion towards your goals.

Fear is also the reaction responsible for the fight-or-flight response, which comes from our amygdala in our "lizard" brains. When you're in fight-or-flight mode, there's no way to reason your way out of it. Your reasoning center, the prefrontal cortex, is offline while the amygdala is active. You won't be able to make good decisions during this time.

. . .

DEACTIVATE THE FIGHT-OR-FLIGHT RESPONSE

At the moment, there are some ways to soothe the amygdala, so it doesn't feel so threatened. Then, your body will stop releasing stress hormones like cortisol, and you can bring your frontal lobes back into play and deal with the issue in a rational way.

The first thing to do is to recognize that your brain is feeling threatened. Remember, it can't tell the difference between a tiger and a big drop in the stock market. Feel the stress hormones, notice your heart pounding, if that's what it takes to identify what's going on.

Then begin to take calm, deep breaths.[1] Only deep breaths have the power to bring down the stress response; fast breathing only reminds your body that it's threatened. There are a few ways to do this, so use whichever works for you. One is known as the "3x3." Inhale for three counts, hold for three counts, exhale for three counts, and repeat three times. (The counting will also help you bring your rational thinking into play.)

Another technique is called "box breathing." Depending on your lung power, hold for a count of three each time. Or even better, a count of five.

Inhale, hold, exhale, hold. Do this several times, and you'll feel yourself relaxing slowly.

When you recognize that you're feeling frightened and not for a good physical reason like someone's chasing you down a dark alley, you can also try acting 'as if.' We discussed this earlier in the context of acting as if you had already achieved your success. In the case of fear, you can try acting as if you aren't afraid.

Note that this is not the same thing as pretending you're not scared. That doesn't help because you won't be able to recognize when your rational mind has gone offline, and the amygdala has taken over.

Instead, you understand that you're feeling a certain way, but you ask yourself how someone who did not have this particular fear would act.

For example, you might be feeling fear before a big presentation. You definitely want to be thinking reasonably when you're doing something like that. Consider your breathing and ask what a confident presenter would be doing.

They would probably be standing straight up, shoulders back, looking confident. You actually don't have to feel or be self-assured to look that way. Such a person would not be holding their papers like a shield in front of their chest and might be taking a small sip of water to ease dry mouth before they got on stage. You can do all that too.

HEADING OFF THE FEAR BEFORE THE LIZARD BRAIN Gets Into the Act

Even better than bringing your rational mind into the picture is preventing it from being hijacked in the first place! There are several techniques that can help you master your fear and prevent it from getting in your way.

1. Visualize not being afraid in a scenario you ordinarily find scary.

Being able to see yourself being successful is such a great technique, and here is another excellent place to practice it. Dread presentations? Imagine yourself doing the entire thing unafraid, from walking confidently on the stage to delivering it and looking at your audience directly as you do so. Then imagine yourself taking questions and knowing the answers so that you respond with confidence. Visualize the entire scenario.Planning to run a marathon, and you're afraid an old injury might pop back up? First, you need to make sure that your training program either has no effect or strengthens your injury. Then, see yourself starting the race, running through the mile markers, and finishing uninjured.

2. Eat the Frightening Frog Directly.

Frogs in the shape of fears, never go away. In fact, when you don't confront them, they simply grow bigger and stronger. A fear frog that may have started out as a regular-size frog will grow every time you shy away from confronting it until the thing is the size of Godzilla.

It's much easier to tackle it when it's small. Again, you need to recognize that you have this fear in order to confront it and prevent it from growing. Being in denial about a very real emotion that you have, in this case, fear, is not going to get you to success.

See it, recognize it, then confront it. If you're afraid of public speaking, and many people are, volunteer to present your team's conclusions at the next business meeting. Even if you fumble a bit, colleagues (and supervisors) will respect that you volunteered.

If that's too much frog to eat in one go, try a speaking group like Toastmasters. They're designed to help people deal with the issue of public speaking. You can normally choose your own topic, so you can at least get started with something you're more comfortable with.[2]

3. Eat the Frightening Frog Repeatedly.

Another way that fear tends to grow is if it's only confronted once. Most of the time, if it's enough of a problem that it's stopping you in your tracks, one try is not enough. You need to repeat daily habits for a time until your brain knows that a certain time of day (or a certain trigger) means it's exercise time.

Similarly, the brain needs repeats until it's comfortable that no, it's not actually going to die when you get up in front of an audience. Some people who really want to write a bestseller are afraid of the blank page (or blank screen for those who type their first drafts). Not much can be done about that but to sit your butt down in a chair in front of a blank page day after day.

Consistently eat the frog, and over time your brain recognizes that the frog will not kill it or harm it in some way. In fact, over time, it might actually seem pretty tasty!

. . .

4. Rinse and repeat.

The more you move toward your fears, and the more you act as if you're unafraid, the more success you'll have. Your brain will be accustomed to the fact that yes, sometimes things are a little scary, especially when they're new and/or unknown. However, now that it's been through a number of frightening scenarios and came out unscathed, it's less likely to freak out when something out of the ordinary happens.

You'll know that you're capable of handling things. How do you know? Well, you've handled them! That's proof for yourself that you can do it. You may find it helpful to write down all of these successes: the wins you had at Toastmasters, the compliment you received from the boss when you gave a great presentation.

Then, on days when everything seems to be going wrong or nothing's going your way, you can look at your list and remind yourself. Yes, you've been here before, and yes, you made it through. If you've done it in the past, there's no reason you can't do it again in the future.

. . .

BE RELENTLESS

There's no reason, especially with all of the habits you've already put in place, to let anything stop you.

"In real life, being relentless is a state of mind that can give you the strength to achieve, survive, to overcome, to be strong when others are not. It means craving the end result so intensely that the work becomes irrelevant. Not just in sports, but in everything you do. The ability to be relentless is in all of us." -Tim Grover[3]

Sounds awesome, but how do you go about it? Fortunately, if you've implemented the tools in this book, you have some routines that take away unnecessary decision-making and support your willpower. Now you just need to expand on them a bit.

1. Take ownership.

Everything in your life is your responsibility. Accidents and incidents happen, and we don't always know why, and we may not be the cause. That's immaterial. How we live our lives and how we choose to deal with adversity is entirely up to us.

Some of us had bad childhoods with parents who didn't support us or actively harmed us in some way. That isn't our fault. However, our parents are not going to be able to fix it or work through the damage. We're the only ones who can do that. If it takes going to a counselor, then go to a counselor.

The past can't be undone, but your actions, words, and thoughts are what determine your present, which in turn determines your future. Think positively, speak affirmatively, and act in ways that keep you in motion towards your goals. That's how you will achieve success.

Blaming your parents, your spouse, your friends, and the universe has no effect on them whatsoever and can prevent you from achieving your goals. You are where and what you are because of you and you only! Own the responsibility that your life is yours to make something out of.

2. Do the work; there are no shortcuts.

The Internet is full of hacks, tips, and tricks. Unfortunately, when it comes to success, the only way to get there is to do the actual work. Sometimes, it seems like people are successful out of nowhere, but they're not. They worked hard, sometimes in obscurity, before they hit the limelight.

Want to lose weight? A concoction of syrup, lemon juice, and water isn't going to help you drop the pounds and keep them off for any length of time. The work to overhaul your diet and include more exercise will, although that won't happen overnight either, as much as we might want it to.

3. Go through the discomfort.

Have you heard the expression, "The only way out is through?" It's easy to get stuck or stopped, especially when you're doing something that's way out of your comfort zone. How tempting to say, "I can't," and go back to your "old" life, the one you were trying to change in the first place, the one that wasn't helping you maximize your potential, the one that kept you fat and if not happy, at least comfortable.

When you want to achieve success, when you have a big goal that you are determined to reach, the only way to get past discomfort is to go through it. Otherwise, you're just turning back—and turning your back on—your path.

Growth doesn't come when you keep doing the comfortable things. It only arrives with hard work and discomfort. If you don't push your boundaries, you're never going to push past them. Want to sit in the back during the team presentation and not say anything? Sit where people can see you and speak up anyway.

Don't want to run that 5-mile loop? Do it anyway. Feeling like the slice of cake has your name on it? Erase your name from it and ignore it. When you give in to the easy life, pretty soon, you're right back to where you started, wishing you had a better life and not doing anything about it.

Is that where you want to be? Of course not, otherwise you wouldn't be reading this book! Take that next uncomfortable step. The only way out of discomfort is through.

Know Your Why

One of the things that helps people push past discomfort is knowing *why* they're trying to reach their goal. You need a good reason that will help you keep going when the obstacles in front of you make you want to give up.

For example, if your goal is to lose weight, looking

good isn't enough of a reason to keep you going through the plateaus that inevitably occur. It's not enough to keep you focused when there's a tempting plate of your favorite cookies at the networking mixer when you're nervous enough about talking to people you don't already know.

You may have heard advice about focusing on the goal of lowering your blood sugar so you're no longer pre-diabetic or improving your cholesterol. Certainly worthy goals, but I don't think they're enough either. Lowering cholesterol is great, but it might not make you feel so good that you're willing to endure the discomfort of ignoring your favorite cookies.

What might be enough: wanting to stay healthy enough that you can see your kids at graduation or walk them down the aisle at their weddings, feeling light enough on your feet that you can chase the grandkids around the yard or take them to the park, not being out of breath walking from the store to your car, or up the three flights from the garage to your office, or feeling confident in yourself to go out on dates and have a fabulous time, even though your ex left you for a younger person.

It's the same for any other goal. Why do you want to

run a marathon? Or climb a mountain? "Because it's there" isn't a good enough reason to do it when there are obstacles and cookies in the way. It may be that you were unathletic as a kid, and you want to prove to yourself (and everyone who knows you) that you can do it. That's a great motivation to get out of your warm bed on a cold morning and start the day's training session.

Why do you want to run your own business? Maybe you just can't stand to abide by other people's rules, especially when those rules seem meaningless or even counterproductive. Or maybe you feel like teammates are dragging you down, and you could soar if it was just you. Are you an introvert who doesn't want to deal with other people all day and would rather write or consult? As you can see, there are plenty of different motivations for the goals that you're seeking. Strong intent is based on emotions because our emotions are what drives decision-making.

How Do You Find Your Why?

Some of you might already know your why or be able to dig past the surface reason of "I want to look good" or "I'm running the marathon because it's there."

If not, look at your list of goals that you have written down and identify every single possible benefit from each goal. Don't worry about whether the benefits are strong enough to keep you going at this point; just write down every single thing you can think of that will be a benefit to you from achieving the goal.

Suppose you're dying to write a bestselling book. What are the benefits of doing so? Some might be process-oriented:

- Force me to write every day.
- Get better at grammar and sentence structure basics.
- Show me that I can achieve my goal of writing 100+ pages.
- Improve my organization in writing.
- Prove everyone who said I couldn't do it was wrong.

OTHER REASONS MIGHT BE MORE OUTCOME-oriented:

- I will have something that lives on after me.
- My name will be on an actual book cover.
- I'll be famous when I'm on the bestseller list.
- My book will get me access to celebrities.
- My book will get me access to more speaking opportunities and/or other work.

You can probably think of others as well. Once you've done this exercise, you can look back at them and see if any of them are motivators for you. Will improving your language basics get you out of the warm bed on a cold morning? Probably not. Which means you need to peel back one more layer.

For each benefit you've listed, write down why it is important. Why is being forced to write every day a benefit? Because it provides you a routine that you can rely on. Next, why is getting better at grammar important? Maybe you want to make sure that all your communications, no matter whether it's a book, email, or social media post, are correct, so people will listen to what you have to say. That might be a little closer, but still not enough.

Why is it important that you show yourself you can write 100+ pages? Because all your life, you were told you'd never amount to anything, but you knew there was something in you that would make you successful. You could take your book and shove it in the face of everyone who thought differently!

Now we're getting to some good, strong motivators. Proving that you can do it when you have naysayers in your life is often just the kick in the pants. You need to sit down and write your thousand words a day. Even after you've found a good motivation, continue down your list of benefits and find a reason behind each. You might end up with several good motivators that will help you push through the discomfort.

Once you've got your why(s), write them down and keep them in places where you can see and/or refer to them often. When an unexpected obstacle suddenly pops up in front of your face, reach for your list. Remind yourself why you're trying to achieve this goal in the first place.

How Badly Do You Want It?

Now that you know why you can throw yourself into the goal. If you only kind of want success, then you won't achieve it. Not willing to skip happy hour every night? Decided you'll spend the weekends "relaxing," meaning drinking and/or partying? Okay with going out to the mall for randomly browsing and buying anything that catches your eye?

You're not going to achieve your goals. It doesn't matter what the goal is; if there are other things you want more, you will not reach it. Beyonce has spent days on set and forgotten to eat because she was so focused on what she was doing.[4]

There are no excuses on the road to success! You put in the work that keeps you on your journey, or you don't, and you get left behind. You are either performing the habits that are bringing you closer to your goal or you're not. You're either getting up to do those long runs in preparation for the marathon... or you're not. Your butt's in the chair pounding out the daily word count, or it isn't, which means your bestseller will never be written. You're staying late after work to polish the presentation you're giving in the morning to make it the best it can be in front of your boss and their boss, or you're at happy hour, which means you're not giving a great presentation and no one is going to be impressed with you.

If you don't want it badly enough, the rest doesn't really matter, because you will give up when things start getting hard, as they always do. When you run into a challenge for one of the other six habits, you won't be able to meet that challenge. The first day you go off your eating plan, you figure, "Well, that's it," and never return to it.

It's All Up to You

Some people find the notion that their success lies entirely within them a little scary! Others may find it liberating. If you need to recognize this fear and devise ways to conquer it, we've got the ingredients for that earlier in this chapter. No one has as much influence over your own success as you do.

Yes, luck plays a part. Nevertheless, when you consistently perform these habits over time, you'll be better able to spot opportunities when they come up. You will believe you can do it, and you have the habits that will help you to reach your goals. The occasional run of bad luck may slow you down, but it doesn't have to stop you.

Why People Fail

There are lots of goals and lots of people who don't

reach their goals. You don't have to become one of them. There are a handful of reasons behind most people's failure to achieve their quest. All you need to do is be aware of them and work to head them off if you see one of these reasons start to rear its ugly head.

1. Don't know why.

If you've gone through the exercise above, this one shouldn't be a problem for you. Once you have at least one strong emotional reason to achieve your goal, you have a way to power through the difficulties you'll encounter along the way.

This deep "why" helps you understand what the purpose of your goal truly is. Your goal is a function of your emotional attachment to your why. It's not about the number of pounds you're losing each week or in total. It's really about the life you want to lead, and the goals you've set are the way you've chosen to get there.

Similarly, writing a book is only tangentially related to the number of words on the page. It's about being a writer and living the life of a writer, whatever that might mean to you. Being a CEO, COO, or CIO isn't about which three letters you want in your title; it's about how you want to shape a particular policy, department, or company.

Being an entrepreneur, for most of us, is really about freedom. The freedom to choose our own goals to work toward the freedom of choosing a schedule that works with our own biological and circadian rhythms.

Sometimes, it's also about the specific product or service you'd like to provide. For someone who's very concerned about climate change, creating buildings or machines that run on solar or wind power might be very important and not a goal at any existing company.

2. Spend too much time on what you don't want, as opposed to what you do want.

Knowing that you want to be self-employed because you don't like running on someone else's schedule won't tell you what kind of service you should offer or what type of company you should start. If all you can think about is not wanting to be fat, that doesn't necessarily tell you which actions to take to achieve that goal.

Successful people know what they actually want, which means they can plan for it. They can work backward from their goal to figure out the steps they need to take every year, quarter, month, week, and day.

It's hard to develop a plan for something you don't want. If you don't know more than to not sit on the sofa every night, it's going to be tough to discover the alternatives. However, when you know you want to spend more time with your family, bingo: now you can put into place whatever steps you need to make it happen.

Focusing on what you don't want—micromanaging supervisors, a tight schedule you have no control over, projects you have no say in, 50 pounds of excess weight, etc.—keeps you looking at the negative. Not only can this lead to loss of confidence, but it also prevents you from looking to the future.

Considering only the things you don't want keeps you stuck in the past. Your goals are ahead of you. When you're driving to a certain destination, like the grocery store, the park, or the hotel where you're going to spend the weekend, what do you look for most of the trip?

Through the windshield to see what's coming up, or in the rear-view mirror, to see what you've passed?

You're looking ahead to the future. You've passed what's in the past already. You might take a quick look in the rearview now and then, but your focus is on the road in front of you.

It's the same with success. Continually looking back is much more likely to result in a wreck. You won't see what's in front of you, and you might run off the road to your goals entirely.

It's important to keep looking forward to make sure you're staying on the path to get where you want to go. If there's an obstacle in your way, you have time to avoid it or go around it. That's also the way you'll spot any opportunities that might present themselves by not looking back.

We've discussed how important it is to have a positive outlook in order to reach your goals. Keeping your attention trained on what you don't want counteracts your positive messaging. Affirmations, positive beliefs, and underlying confidence that you can, indeed, complete your quest are how you'll reach your goals, not by taking too much time on the obstacles, the excuses, and the negativity.

3. Get overwhelmed and/or take on too much.

Many people don't take the steps outlined in this

book, and so they try to do too much at once. 26.2 miles is a long distance to cover, especially if you're out of breath walking around the block right now. That goal may seem way too overwhelming, and so it gets dropped.

Or, it seems like a big goal, and a potential marathon runner who hasn't run for fifteen years decides they need to get out there and tackle it. They attempt to run ten miles a day every day. It's no surprise when they get hurt pretty quickly and then drop the goal.

Practicing the habits in this book will help prevent you from being overwhelmed and from taking on too much. You know that you need to take small steps, even if the journey seems like a long one. You take on one new habit at a time and make sure that it gets ingrained before you tackle another one.

Someone who hasn't run for fifteen years but is in otherwise good shape might choose to jog for a few minutes every day just to get their body used to run again. They won't start increasing mileage until jogging feels natural. Someone who's not in very good shape, to begin with, might start with a walk around the block after dinner with their spouse and kids and build up from there.

Your own personal goals and how far along the path you are already will dictate what the steps are that you start with. But however far along you are, it's important to take goals and habits one at a time and start small. That's how good habits get built, and the risk of doing too much and getting overwhelmed is decreased.

Chapter Summary

- Fear is a common obstacle to success.
- At the moment, practice deep breathing and act as if you're not scared.
- Prevent the fear by recognizing it and visualizing otherwise scary scenarios where you triumph.
- Work to minimize the fear by confronting it head-on and doing so consistently.
- The key to achieving your goals is to be relentless.
- Take ownership of your life and goals.
- Do the work; there are no shortcuts to success.
- The only way out of the discomfort is through it.

- Know why you want to reach your goal so that you can overcome temporary difficulties and obstacles along the way.
- These motivations must be strong and contain some kind of emotional tie.
- If you don't know what your "why" is, look at your goals and brainstorm all of the benefits from reaching that goal you can think of. Then, go through each benefit and decide why it's important.
- Write down all of the benefits and motivators.
- When you find strong emotional motivators, write them down and post them in places you will easily see and refer to them.

AFTERWORD

Now you've learned the seven most important habits to achieve your goals. It doesn't matter which specific goal you're trying to achieve because all these routines are key to understand what your goals are and to support your determination to accomplish what you set out to do.

Remember that the actual implementation of them is what keeps you on a successful path. It's great to imagine yourself conquering your fears or overcoming something that has always been a sticking point for you, but more important is doing the work to make these things happen. Unfortunately, there are no shortcuts to success. While this book provides some tips and tricks to help you set habits and routines in place, you will still need to work hard and make some sacrifices in order to get what you want.

Pop culture and the media don't help. We're inundated with clickbait articles that promise quick or easy success. We celebrate athletes, best-selling novelists, and jewelry designers who appear to have come out of nowhere. Instant gratification is baked into American culture.

You don't see the hours that the athletes put in at the gym, and you don't see the failures they endured over the years as younger players. You don't see the novelist sitting in front of the computer for hours on end every single day, and you might not be aware of the several novels that they wrote before the bestseller because you never heard of them. You don't see the time the jewelry designer spent at a magazine editing jewelry features or the hours behind the department store counter.

Nonetheless, that doesn't mean they weren't there. You didn't see all the happy hours that the athlete skipped because they were in the gym, practicing basic skills over and over and over. You didn't see the weekends given up to writing or pitching the novel. The point is, just because you don't see the sacrifices that successful people have made doesn't mean they weren't made.

The journey to success usually doesn't happen overnight. There's a lot of blood, sweat, and tears that go into these endeavors. It takes time to implement the habits, to set up the routines, and take the necessary steps. You will need to work hard. You'll also need to work smart, which is what the habits in this book will help you with.

Naturally, in any journey, there are ups, downs, and obstacles that you must conquer to reach your ultimate destination. This is where many people fail because they don't put routines in place that help them over these bumps in the road. Implementing the seven habits we've discussed puts you on the road to success. For each one, you now have tips on how to put them into place.

The most fundamental habit of all seven is the first, which is to create a powerful foundation based on mindset. You won't be able to achieve success if you don't believe you can. Without the proper mindset, you will not reach your destination. Thinking positively about yourself and your capabilities, and surrounding yourself with other positive thinkers, is the first step on the ladder to success.

Secondly, self-discipline is the key to achievement. There are ways to strengthen and build your supply of this important characteristic, as well as methods to help support it. Habit 3 focuses on how to set goals that you can accomplish. Short and medium-term habits and goals help you reach your ultimate success.

Creating routines (Habit 4) helps you stay on your journey by automating certain small habits that you need to succeed. That way, you don't have to rely so much on willpower and self-discipline alone. It takes a while to successfully implement a routine because it must be done one step at a time. Once it's in place, you free yourself up to do the necessary hard work.

Fifth, being able to manage interpersonal relationships is important for your goals. Acquiring a mentor is crucial for your journey, and how to build trust isn't always obvious. In addition, you may need partners and peers to support you on your path, and you want to manage those relationships effectively.

Habit 6 is all about how to maintain good physical health through nutrition. This may be clear when your goal is physical, but what if it isn't? It turns out the brain and body are highly interconnected. If you want your brain to be at optimum performance, you need to feed it and the rest of your body well.

The good news is that you don't have to buy pricey new cleanses and toxin removers or the latest new superfood from the wilds of Antarctica. There are some foods that are especially good for your brain, which are discussed in this chapter, but mainly you just need to fill your basket with food as close to its natural state as possible.

Finally, in Chapter 7, we discuss the motivation behind staying on that path to success and not turning back when the going gets tough. You need to know why your goal is so important, be relentless in reaching for it, and stop making excuses. Discomfort is the only way to grow, so pushing through it is the only way for you to win.

Reading about these habits is great but won't get you any farther ahead on your journey. In order to actually get to where you want to go, you have to take action. Write down the affirmations and put them where you'll see them every day. Evaluate your daily activities and, more importantly, remove or decrease the ones that aren't proactively pushing you forward.

You have to eat the walnuts, not just read about them being good sources of omega-3 fats. You'll need to physically put your phone down and charge it in another room to spend more quality time with your family and to get more quality sleep. You must write down your motivation for reaching your goal —and if you can't, go through the exercise in Chapter 7 to figure it out.

The habits discussed here are based on science, what is known about the brain, the body, and the psychology behind why we do what we do. Why do so many people fail to achieve their goals or maintain them consistently?

Research shows us why sleep is so important. A better understanding of the brain-body feedback loop helps us determine how to bring rational thought back online when fear threatens to overwhelm us and to eat foods that are important for proper functioning. In other words, though habits are widely discussed in popular media and entertainment, these are backed by research.

If you can take only one thing away from this book (and I certainly hope you take more than that!), understand the power of your mind in any kind of success. Everyone has bad luck now and then or gets a raw deal. Using your mind efficiently and effectively will help you get over these times and the obstacles that you'll encounter. Simply setting your mind to positivity will help you accomplish more than any seminar or motivational speaker. The power is within you, so use it to your benefit.

Lead the life you've always wanted!

RESOURCES

1. HABIT 1 - CREATE A POWERFUL FOUNDATION

1. https://www.briantracy.com/blog/personal-success/positive-attitude-happy-people-positive-thinking/
2. https://edison.rutgers.edu/newsletter9.html
3. https://www.streetdirectory.com/travel_guide/8799/self_improvement_and_motivation/your_mindset_determines_your_success_in_life.html
4. https://www.entrepreneur.com/article/308843

2. HABIT 2 - THE IMPORTANT ROLE OF SELF-DISCIPLINE

1. https://positivepsychology.com/delayed-gratification/
2. https://jamesclear.com/delayed-gratification

3. HABIT 3 - LET'S SET THE GOALS

1. https://www.briantracy.com/blog/personal-success/success-through-goal-setting-part-1-of-3/

4. HABIT 4 - CREATING A ROUTINE AND STICKING TO IT

1. https://www.inc.com/melody-wilding/psychology-says-this-is-how-you-change-a-bad-habit-for-good.html
2. https://www.bbc.com/news/technology-44640959
3. https://www.fastcompany.com/90415438/yes-social-media-is-making-you-miserable
4. https://www.rush.edu/health-wellness/discover-health/why-you-should-eat-breakfast
5. https://www.critcaremd.com/wp-content/up-loads/2017/07/Healthy_sleep_in_adults.pdf
6. https://www.entrepreneur.com/article/344178
7. https://www.entrepreneur.com/article/344178
8. https://www.entrepreneur.com/article/249387
9. https://www.sleepfoundation.org/articles/why-electronics-may-stimulate-you-bed

5. HABIT 5 - LISTEN TO BUILD STRONG RELATIONSHIPS

1. https://www.straitstimes.com/opinion/learning-to-see-things-from-anothers-perspective

6. HABIT 6 - EAT WELL, LIVE AMAZING

1. https://www.brainfacts.org/ask-an-expert/how-does-the-brain-use-food-as-energy
2. https://www.healthline.com/nutrition/sugar-and-inflam-mation#section3

3. https://www.medicalnewstoday.com/arti-cles/325919.php#is-diet-soda-bad-for-you
4. https://www.medicalnewstoday.com/articles/325325.php#1
5. https://www.indiahomehealthcare.com/blogpost/the-importance-of-water-in-our-daily-lives/
6. https://www.theglobeandmail.com/life/health-and-fitness/ask-a-health-expert/which-is-healthier-tea-or-coffee/article546635/
7. https://www.healthline.com/nutrition/11-brain-foods

7. HABIT 7 - PUSH YOURSELF HARDER THAN ANYONE ELSE

1. https://www.healthline.com/health/stress/amygdala-hijack#how-to-stop
2. https://www.toastmasters.org/
3. https://www.inc.com/julian-hayes-ii/elon-musk-and-michael-jordan-can-teach-you-to-be-s.html
4. http://placeofpersistence.com/motivation-lessons-from-how-bad-do-you-want-it-videos/